you&your

MINI

NEW

DISCARDED

you&your

NEW MINI

Tim Mundy *Buying, enjoying, maintaining, modifying*

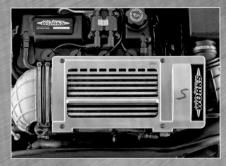

© Tim Mundy 2004

First published in September 2004

Tim Mundy has asserted his right to
be identified as the author of this work.

British Library cataloguing-in-publication data:
A catalogue record for this book is available
from the British Library

Published by Haynes Publishing,
Sparkford, Yeovil, Somerset BA22 7JJ, UK

Tel: 01963 442030 Fax: 01963 440001
Int. tel: +44 1963 442030 Int. fax: +44 1963 440001
E-mail: sales@haynes-manuals.co.uk
Web site: www.haynes.co.uk

ISBN 1 84425 028 8

Library of Congress catalog card no. 2004104456

Haynes North America, Inc.,
861 Lawrence Drive, Newbury Park,
California 91320, USA

Designed by G&M Designs Limited,
Raunds, Northamptonshire
Printed and bound in Great Britain by
J. H. Haynes & Co. Ltd, Sparkford

Contents

Acknowledgements

Many people have helped me in putting together this book. My grateful thanks go to them all. Although, sadly, it would be impossible to mention everybody by name, those who I feel deserve a special mention are as follows:

Natalie Wakefield and Elyssia Graymore at BMW GB

Mike Cooper and Richard de Jong at John Cooper Works

Nathan King and the staff at North Oxford Garage

Monty Watkins, Karen Drury and Paul Wiltshire at *MiniWorld* magazine

Everyone at Mini Spares, Mini Sport and Minispeed.

Introduction

Minis are simply unique. The original Mini was, and still is, an icon, held in warm affection by people around the world, a jaunty symbol of its era – and 42 years after the introduction of the first model the New Mini looks like getting the same devoted following. It has retained the feel and character of its predecessor, yet quickly established a personality in its own right too.

This is a car that exists not only to provide safe,

The New Mini, a superb combination of legendary breeding and modern technical sophistication. (BMW Press)

reliable and comfortable transport but also sets out to be enjoyed. The New Mini can be driven in standard form, which is a pleasing experience, but you can also personalise it with accessories or modified components from BMW, with one of the John Cooper Works packages or some of the increasing number of aftermarket parts that are available. The old Mini was a very hard act to follow: not only was it technically very innovative at the time, but it also appealed across a wide social spectrum. The New Mini does this too. Popular from launch, it is loved by the vast majority, and to the few who do not appreciate it, I can only advise a test drive – almost always this results in a favourable opinion.

I grew up from the age of three with a Mini in the family. My own proper 'hands on' involvement with Minis began in my early teens and it continues to this day. Like millions of others in Britain and around the world, I chose a Mini as my first car, and I eagerly awaited the coming of the new model. At the time of writing the New Mini is three years old and over the coming decade or two it will no doubt become the first car of many more people as they reach driving age. In many cases it will also become their second and third car and so on because the whole Mini thing is addictive. Having once owned a Mini, people tend not to want to be without one.

The New Mini has sold 500,000 already and 175,000 will be built in 2004. It not only secures the future for the whole Mini scene but makes it a whole lot brighter in the process, for all the models are excellent cars.

This book sets out to give an overview of the New Mini, it gives an insight into the wonderful history leading up to its creation and shows how to improve the car and generally get a whole lot more out of it than even the manufacturer envisaged. Hopefully above all it will enable you to enjoy your New Mini to the full.

Tim Mundy
August 2004

The Convertible looks cool from any angle.

Chapter One

Genesis and evolution

Considering the huge number of makes and models of car that have been available in over 100 years of motoring, truly legendary cars are really quite few and far between. Although there have been, and currently are, a number of really good cars, there are only a handful that really stand apart from the rest. Some examples that immediately spring to mind, in no particular order, include the Model T Ford, VW Beetle, Citroën 2CV, Land Rover, Austin 7, and, in more recent times, the VW Golf. But to me, and many, many others, there is one car that stands out above all of these. It is the Mini.

Launched back in August 1959, discontinued in 2000, and reborn as a totally new vehicle in 2001, the Mini is without question Britain's most remarkable car. Loved by virtually everyone, it has played a part at some point in the lives of the majority of the population of the United Kingdom, and a great many people in other parts of the world too. The original Mini won many awards, and has been voted Car of the Century by *Autocar* magazine, and Best European Car of the Century in Las Vegas, coming second overall in the latter only to the Model T Ford. These are quite remarkable achievements.

The original Mini was in production for 41 years, and any successor to the original design therefore had a lot to live up to, for many reasons. Perhaps first and foremost it had to be different from anything else on the road: the original Mini really was different, and managed to remain so throughout the whole of its production life. Many manufacturers copied the design principle, and although there were a number of other good small cars, such as the Fiat 500 (in itself an Italian icon), nothing really ever came close to the particular individuality that the Mini exuded. Another absolute requirement of a new Mini was that it would have to

have fantastic handling, the type of handling that puts a smile on the face of the driver, and more often than not the passengers' faces too. Most of all it must have the overall cheekiness, the unique individuality coupled with appeal, that simply makes it a Mini.

The new Mini – the BMW Mini – was launched in 2001, having been more eagerly awaited, perhaps, than any other new car ever. And when it finally arrived some months after the demise of the first Mini, the New Mini was rapturously received by both the public and the press. Rightly so, for it managed to achieve all those criteria that entitled it to justly wear the Mini badge. The road by which it came into being, however, was a long and at times a somewhat bumpy one.

Ancestry

Although this book is about the New Mini, we must first take a look at the Mini family tree, for this is important, not only as a major part of motoring history but also in order to understand why BMW wanted the Mini. The Mini name takes a lot of living up to.

The original Mini is almost certainly unique in that it was made by a great many different 'companies' during its lifetime. Although badged Austin and Morris, with Wolseley and Riley derivatives, the Mini was first made by The British Motor Corporation (BMC). This was followed in 1968 by British Leyland, then Leyland Cars,

DID YOU KNOW?

The first milestone for the old Mini was reached in December 1962, when the 500,000th rolled off the line three years and four months after the car was launched. The New Mini achieved its own half-million in August 2004, just over three years and two months after launch.

An early ancestor. This is a 1964 Morris Mini Minor Super DeLuxe.

Austin Rover, Rover Group, and BMW. After this, it was made by MG Rover under licence from BMW. In a strange and roundabout way this could be considered to be full circle, as what is often forgotten is that there was a link between BMW and Austin many years ago which involved the car that was without a doubt the original ancestor of the Mini. This was also the car from which early Austin Mini's took their name: the Austin Seven.

The BMW link occurred in the 1920s when the Austin Motor Company began selling a few Sevens to Germany, where they were very well received. Sir Herbert Austin, founder of the company, decided that rather than face possible problems with currency fluctuation and import restrictions his best way forward would be to sell the manufacturing rights of the Austin Seven to a German company. A deal was struck with a company named Dixi, and in late 1927 production of the car, pure Austin Seven but named Dixi, started. After the initial production run Dixi began making their own version, the Dixi DA-1, and before the end of 1928 some 6,000 cars had been sold.

In late 1928 Dixi became a subsidiary of BMW AG and the DA-1 was renamed the BMW Dixi. In 1929 the Dixi name was dropped and the car was then known as the BMW 3/15 DA-2. The very first BMW model rolled off the line on 22 March 1929, with a 750cc engine producing 15hp. Throughout its production life many parts were modified, but its Austin Seven origins remained clearly visible. A further 19,000 cars were produced up until the end of 1932 when production ceased.

Back in Britain the next forerunner to the Mini was the Austin A30/A35. Designed by Dick Burzi and launched at the 1951 Motor Show, the Austin A30 Seven was the long awaited replacement for the Austin Seven, which had by then been out of production for 12 years. The A30 is particularly significant in the story as it was the first car to be fitted with the A Series engine – which was, in fact, developed specifically for the A30. In September 1956 the A30 was superseded by the A35, a car which looked very similar and was in reality a Mark 2 version of the A30. It was distinguished primarily by its painted radiator grille and larger rear window. The A35 retained the A Series engine, but the capacity was increased to 948cc; 848cc and 1,098cc A Series engines were also fitted to various derivatives

Classic interior provided seating for four in a reasonable degree of comfort for the time. This car has the 'magic wand' gear lever.

of the A35. The A35 itself was discontinued when the original Mini was introduced.

The Morris Minor also played a part in the history of the Mini. It was designed by Alec Issigonis, and although when launched it was fitted with the 918cc side-valve engine from the Morris Eight Series E it gained the A Series engine in 1953. Another point worth noting, which is very relevant to the Mini story, is that Issigonis first experimented with front-wheel drive in a specially built Morris Minor.

In 1956 Issigonis was working for BMC, a company which was formed when Austin and Morris merged in 1952. The brief to design the Mini came about as a result of fuel shortages due to the Suez crisis in 1957, when Egypt nationalised the Suez Canal and disrupted oil supplies to the West. Fuel rationing was introduced limiting an individual's supply to between six and 10½ gallons a month, depending upon the engine capacity of their car. As a result a number of 'bubble cars' started to appear on the roads. These were very small and economical low cost cars fitted with what were basically motorcycle engines. BMC's Managing Director Leonard Lord told Alec Issigonis to design a car to 'knock all the bubble cars off the road'. Perhaps

the most interesting twist to this story is that one of the most popular bubble cars was the Isetta, which was built by BMW, so it could be argued that in a roundabout way BMW were partly responsible for the original Mini being designed in the first place …

Issigonis's brief was to design a people's car, an economical runabout which would seat four adults and carry their luggage in comfort, a car which would bring motoring to the masses. The target market for the car was the 'flat caps', the British working class (in the 1950s the home market was the main market). After a very brief development period the Mini was launched on 26 August 1959. Very different to all other cars available at the time, the Mini's revolutionary compactly packaged, transverse-engined, front-wheel drive layout was to ultimately become adopted by virtually every motor manufacturer in the world. What's more, the design principle would in fact become the layout for the majority of new cars 30 or so years later.

Although it is universally accepted that the Mini started the front-wheel drive revolution, it is important

The central speedometer with oil pressure and water temperature gauges either side.

to point out that other motor manufacturers – notably Citroën and Saab – had produced front-wheel drive cars some years previously. But it was the Mini's transverse engine layout that made the most significant impact. No other car in history has had such a major influence on car design and on motoring in general. Interestingly it has taken a while for this design influence to rub off on BMW, who retain a front inline engine and rear-wheel drive very successfully on all BMW-branded cars to the present day. The New Mini is BMW's first front-wheel drive car, which is probably one of the main reasons why it is marketed as a separate brand.

The New Mini dashboard is based around the original design.

The first Mini was initially available in two versions: the Morris Mini Minor and the Austin Seven. Apart from different badging and radiator grilles, these were basically identical. At the time of their launch Britain was still recovering from the Second World War, which had only ended 14 years previously – to put this in perspective, this is equivalent, at the time of writing, to 1990 (in Britain this is when G or H registration cars were made, and was the year that the Mini Cooper was reintroduced). Although some aspects of life, such as the music scene, were picking up, and there was generally a brighter outlook on the horizon, many everyday things remained somewhat austere. The exterior paintwork on houses was often black or dark brown, clothing was a lot less cheery, and everything was generally a good deal more formal in both appearance and behaviour than it is today. But cars were destined to play an ever increasing role in people's lives from this point on, and the Mini was to play a huge part in this change. It was sold as a family car that had enough room for four people, and although very small by today's standards, in 1959 the car-buying public was used to small cars with limited legroom and small luggage capacity.

The Mini's most notorious feature was its ability to out-corner anything else on four wheels. This meant that anyone could enjoy sports car handling every day as they drove to work, or took the family to see the relatives on a Sunday afternoon – at least the drive would be something to look forward to, even if the visit wasn't! Most road testers raved about the Mini. Its performance was good, and they all acknowledged that the roadholding beat even the best handling sports cars of the time. The Mini was actually described as having 'dart like stability' due to its combination of rack and pinion steering and independent rubber suspension. It really did set new standards in the handling department. There was, for a start, considerably less body roll than with more conventional cars, and the front-wheel drive layout only served to increase the positive feel of the steering. This was all on cross-ply tyres and with single leading shoe front brakes too.

The new BMW Mini is different to anything else on the road. It is a bold and very individual design. In this way it is very much a chip off the old block. In 1959 and the early 1960s the original Mini was considered a strange, ultra-modern design. Many people considered it to be ugly and 'over windowed'. Compared to the 'normal' cars that everybody else was driving it was revolutionary, every bit as much in appearance as in engineering design. This may well have had something to do with the poor sales figures achieved at the beginning of the Mini's life, for there was far greater resistance to new and untried products 45 years ago than there is today. Probably the one saving factor in the original Mini's make up was its tried and tested A Series engine, although even this was transversely mounted and integral with the gearbox, sharing the same oil, whereas previously it had always been fitted in a conventional inline layout. Sales picked up in the 1960s and peaked in the early to mid-1970s.

The Mini was launched at just the right time, for as the 1960s dawned the world was crying out for fun and recovery, and the Mini was the car that was going to play a part in achieving it. At the beginning of the decade cars were not so widely used for commuting, many people going to work instead on a bicycle, which meant that those wealthy enough to own cars kept them in the garage polished up for weekends and holidays. The Mini played a big part in changing this. It was a cheap car which was easy to drive and fitted in well with the social changes that were taking place at the time. The 1960s set the scene for the Mini, with Mini Coopers, famous owners, and outstanding competition successes. This popularity continued through the 1970s and into the early 1980s.

Within a few years of its launch the Mini was, simply, fashion. It had been Issigonis's vision that working-class men would drive his creation, and he was right, they did. But the Mini proved to have a far wider appeal. From very early on in its life it enjoyed ownership among the rich and famous. The list of celebrity owners is endless, and includes Twiggy, Jean Shrimpton, Lulu, Spike Milligan, the Beatles, Peter Sellers, Britt Ekland, Lord Snowdon, Princess Grace of Monaco, Enzo Ferrari, Graham Hill, and Mary Quant (who, in the 1980s, would design the colour scheme of the special edition 'Designer' Mini). It is probably because of this, as much as for any other reason, that the Mini has become a leading symbol of the 1960s. It was a fun car in what were, for many, fun times. There are few folk without some happy memory of the Mini. For many people it was part of growing up; for others it was their first car.

The Mini even started a whole new section in the dictionary. As far as I know it is the only car that has ever managed to do this, with perhaps the most memorable spin-off name being the 'mini skirt'. The two simply went together in the 1960s and early 1970s,

A huge tuning industry grew up around the Mini. This 1,430cc car has much uprated suspension and brakes.

and one advertisement for the Mini even depicted a Mini being 'worn' as a skirt.

With all this behind it, it is hardly surprising that Rover chose, in the later years of the Mini's production, to market it as a fashion statement, the car to be seen in and a plaything for the weekends. It was also part of setting the scene for the introduction of a brand new model.

During its production lifetime the Mini underwent a great deal of change, and effectively seven different 'marks' of Mini were made. The Mark 1, with the rounded 'moustache' radiator grille, lasted until October 1967 (the New Mini's radiator grille is based upon this original design). In the early 1960s the Mini range was widened to include a van and pick up and two estate versions, the Austin Mini Countryman and the Morris Mini Traveller. The best known Minis of all, though, were the Cooper models.

The Cooper connection is very significant in the Mini story. In 1960 John Cooper suggested producing a sports version of the Mini to Alec Issigonis. Issigonis was not particularly excited by the idea, but others within BMC were, and as a result Downton, a company

in the business of tuning exotic cars, started development work. The result was the 997 Cooper launched in 1961, with a 997cc engine, increased in 1964 to 998cc. By 1962 Daniel Richmond had become a consultant engineer to BMC, and was working on the Cooper S engine. The Cooper S arrived in 1963 with a 1,071cc engine. 970cc engined versions were also available for a short time before the capacity was increased to 1,275cc. BMC Special Tuning produced conversion kits, which could be fitted without affecting the car's warranty. Tuning gear was also available from BMC Special Tuning, which became British Leyland Special Tuning in the 1970s. Without the Cooper connection it is highly possible that there would not be a New Mini today.

From the Mini design BMC went on to develop a range of larger family cars, all designed by the Issigonis team. The Austin/Morris 1100, and later the 1300, was always considered the car to progress to when a family outgrew the Mini. It shared the same power train as the Mini, and the 1275 engine from the 1300 was also fitted into the Mini 1275GT. The 1800 was a much larger saloon fitted with the 1,800cc B Series engine, and other badge-engineered versions of both cars were available. There was also the Austin Maxi, available in 1,500 and 1,750cc versions an early five-door

There were many special editions of the original Mini. This one marked 30 years of production in 1989.

hatchback. These cars were the mainstay of BMC and BLMC throughout the 1960s and also into the 1970s.

The Mark 2 Mini, with its bolder, more angular grille and larger rear window, ran from October 1967 until October 1969. The 998 Cooper was also available in Mark 2 guise, as was the 1,275cc Cooper S. The Mark 3 Mini and the Clubman range of two saloon models and an estate were introduced in October 1969. Mark 3 Minis are easily distinguished by their internal door hinges. At this point the 998 Cooper was dropped from the range and replaced by the Clubman fronted Mini 1275GT. The 1275 Cooper S continued in Mark 2 guise until March 1970, when the Mark 3 S was announced. The Cooper S was finally discontinued in July 1971. The Mark 4 Mini of 1976 was similar to the Mark 3 but had rubber mounted subframes. The Mark 5 of 1984 had 12in wheels and front disc brakes.

In the 1980s the Mini resisted its greatest replacement challenge in the form of the Metro, a car which was very successful to start with and hailed as 'The British Car To Beat The World'. It was actually not a bad car, the MG versions being lively and quite fun to drive. They were popular in their day and were at one time quite the car to be seen in, in many ways the same as a New Mini Cooper or S is today. Sadly, the Metro later gained a bad reputation for rust and reliability,

and good A Series engined examples (later Rover Metros were fitted with Rover's K Series engine and the car was renamed the Rover 100 in 1988) are an increasingly rare sight on British roads.

There was a huge Mini 'revival' in 1989 spearheaded by the model's 30th birthday celebrations. The best news of all concerned the relaunch of the Cooper. As the sales brochure accurately said, it could only ever have happened to one car. Plans to reintroduce the Cooper had actually started some years earlier. In 1985, 14 years after the last original S had rolled off the production line, a 998cc Mini was converted by John Cooper Garages and sent to Japan, where interest in the possibility of a new Cooper was very high. This

The Mini Cooper was first reintroduced as a limited edition of 1,000 cars in 1990.

prototype Cooper generated 1,000 orders, and as a result a Cooper conversion kit for the UK was produced in time for the Mini's 30th anniversary. Rover produced the Racing, Flame, and Checkmate Special Edition Minis especially to go with the kit, which was available both from John Cooper and from Rover dealers, as a supply and fit option.

Shortly after this it was agreed that the 1,275cc Mini Cooper would be relaunched. Initially this would be a Rover Special Product, and 1,000 would be produced. These sold immediately, and the mainstream car then went into production. It had also been agreed that an S conversion would be produced by John Cooper, and this too was available through Cooper Garages in Ferring and from Rover dealers. As with the 998 conversion, the S pack was accepted by Rover and carried the full Rover warranty.

This was only really the beginning of the revival story, as, due to stricter emissions regulations, the outlook for the Mini was beginning to look very bleak indeed, and production of all Minis was set to end towards the end of 1991. However, the necessary

development work was carried out to enable production to continue, and as a result all Minis sported a 1,275cc engine. This was the Mark 6. The Mini Cooper was fitted with single point fuel injection, while the non-Cooper models retained a carburettor until 1995. The S option continued, for the injection cars, but was now more comprehensive, and included Koni shock absorbers and wider, lower profile 165/60 x 12 Dunlop tyres. This new S pack was fitted to brand new cars, and this time was only available from John Cooper Garages. The list of available options had also grown and many cars were being fitted with full leather upholstery and other luxuries.

Even stricter emissions regulations were still on the horizon, and Mini production would have ended for certain during 1996 if it had not been for Bernd Pischetsrieder of BMW, who is, incidentally, a distant relative of Alec Issigonis. This time a very considerable sum of money – no one would ever disclose just how much – was spent bringing the Mini into line with both safety and emissions legislation. This second major re-engineering created the Mark 7 Mini. It was still very much a Mini, but now came complete with an airbag and side impact bars. The A Series engine was re-engineered to accept twin point injection, these later engines being easily distinguished by the higher

The A Series engine that powered all original Minis and a number of other BMC cars too. This is a late Mini, with the twin point fuel injection fitted after the final re-engineering.

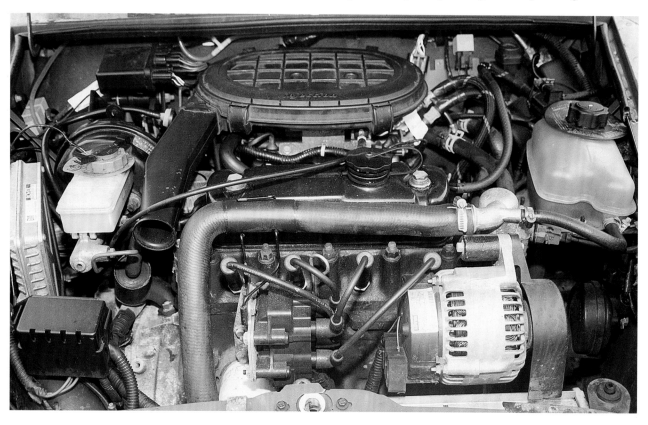

position of the alternator and the lack of a distributor. At this point 13in wheels and Sports Pack wheel arch extensions became optional and were fitted to a large number of Minis. The options list was increased and it was possible to buy a fully personalised Mini direct from Rover rather than buying the car and then spending a fortune on accessories, although of course this was still possible too.

This incarnation of the Mini would almost certainly never have happened if BMW had not bought the Rover Group in 1994. Mini prices rose dramatically, but despite this the revamp could not possibly have been economical in terms of sales. What it was really all about was BMW keeping the Mini alive for the lead up to the launch of the New Mini.

Despite the fact that, in appearance, early Minis are much the same as the last models off the line, very few parts from an original 1959 Mini would, in fact, fit a 2001 production model. For example, the only major body panel that is correct for first and last Minis is the roof.

Apart from the Metro, which was originally designed as a Mini replacement, there were a number of attempts to come up with a new Mini. Perhaps the most notable of these was in 1967, when Issigonis himself started to design a replacement. The new car

was code named 9X. It was to be completely new, with new suspension, engine, and completely redesigned body. Although similar in overall size to the Mini it bore little resemblance to it, but the design was very definitely Issigonis, with strong hints of 1100 and Maxi. Two 9X prototypes were built, of which one still survives. The project was cancelled after the Leyland merger.

In 1994 Rover Advanced Vehicles produced a wider and longer version of the original Mini which was equipped with the K Series engine and Hydragas suspension as fitted to later Metros.

In 1995 interest in the possibility of a new Mini gained pace and Rover produced two concept cars named Spiritual and Spiritual Too. Both were rather oddly shaped, with little bonnet area and a mid-mounted engine. Rover considered that these could be replacements for the Mini, but – thank goodness – BMW did not share their point of view.

The closest concept to the New Mini was the ACV30 built in 1996. This was publicly paraded at the 1997 Monte Carlo Rally along with a trio of 1960s rally-winning Minis. Although not a prototype build of the

Towards the end of its production life, the Mini was marketed under BMW ownership as a fashion accessory with numerous options.

real New Mini there were a number of styling similarities. It must be said, though, that the actual BMW Mini is much better looking.

Early in 2000 BMW decided very abruptly – at least from the point of view of the general public – to dispose of the Rover Group, even if this meant closing it down. Rover was losing too much money for BMW to keep it going. The way that this came about was unfortunate, and at the time generated a lot of anti-BMW feeling, particularly within the UK. Production of the original Mini therefore ended under a cloud, which is a great shame as it tainted the feelings of a number of original Mini enthusiasts towards the new one. Some would probably have felt this way regardless,

being unable to accept the original Issigonis design concept being radically altered to create a new model. But the fact remains that the original Mini needed to be replaced – fantastic though it was and still is, it was dated when compared to cars of the 1990s and the new millennium. No amount of further re-engineering could have kept the Mini going in anything like its original form, and to attempt further development of the existing shape would almost certainly have ruined it anyway.

In October 2000 production of the original Mini came to an end. A total of 5,387,862 Minis had been made during a remarkable 41 years of production. Unusually for a car which had remained in production for so long and maintained basically the same appearance, the original Mini was not on the whole considered an old-fashioned car even towards the end of its life. This was partly due to the ongoing new packaging and engineering which had maintained its trendy image, but it also says a great deal about the timelessness of the design.

For anyone interested in tracing the bloodline of the Mini family a visit to the Heritage Motor Museum at Gaydon makes an excellent day out. A BMW Dixi is also

There is much of the BMW 3 series in the New Mini.

to be found there, as well as a number of different Mini models including 621 AOK (the first ever Mini), a 9X, Monte Carlo winners, the last production Mini, and the first ever BMW Mini off the line, a Mini Cooper. Any Mini enthusiast will find it well worth a visit.

Enter the New Mini

The New Mini was launched in Britain in July 2001. Europe had to wait a little longer, until September, and the United States, Australia, and Japan had to wait until spring 2002 for their New Minis. The first to appear on the scene in Britain were the Mini Cooper and the Mini One, the Cooper being the first to be test driven by the press.

The New Mini was possibly the most eagerly awaited car ever. Test cars had, tantalisingly, been seen for many months, particularly around the Oxford area near the factory. Some had been heavily disguised, others – particularly nearer to the launch date – not so. The design team was led by Frank Stephenson. The fact that quite a lot of New Mini drivers will know this says something about Minis as a whole – how many Vauxhall Astra or Ford Focus drivers, even the enthusiastic ones, would know the name of their cars' designer?

Unlike its predecessor, the New Mini was an immediate sales success, and by the end of 2001 over 11,600 had been registered, almost 20 per cent more than BMW had anticipated. Like its predecessor, though, it set new standards for driver involvement. Build quality was impressive too, being fully up to BMW standards but in a much smaller package than had previously been available. The New Mini was also the first front-wheel drive car ever to be made by BMW, who, although they have made, and continue to make, four-wheel drive cars, are in the main very much committed to rear-wheel drive.

Many of the original Mini design fundamentals are present, but technically the New Mini is very modern and utilises numerous electronic systems. BMW are keen to point out, though, that the Issigonis concept of a wheel at each corner, a low centre of gravity, wide track, and relatively long wheelbase – all vital ingredients of the driving dynamics – are still present.

There are those people who maintain that the New Mini is quite obviously a Mini from an appearance point

The first of the new. This is a pre-production Mini One, photographed at a press launch in the Brecon Beacons in Wales.

Size comparison. The New Mini is quite a bit longer and taller than the old one.

of view 'because it looks exactly like the old one'. This I do not agree with. It is a new design in its own right, although there are a number of features that have been carried over, perhaps the most notable being the bonnet closing line down the side of the wing which replicates the front wing/A panel seam on the old car. Interestingly the 'clamshell' bonnet is effectively a one-piece front end which, although hinged like a traditional bonnet, is similar in principle to the glass fibre front ends fitted by Mini owners in the 1970s to cure rust problems and latterly on modified cars to make for easy access.

Some owners of original Minis are shocked by the differences, but many fail to remember that as the original Mini remained the same shape for 41 years it was not given the chance to evolve gradually in the way that cars such as the VW Golf have done, or even the BMW 3 Series, which is replaced with a new model every seven years. The New Mini had to jump from 1959 to 2001 in one go, and it did so very successfully. In fact this was part of the aim of the design team, to make the car that they felt would have been arrived at anyway if the normal automotive

evolutionary process had been allowed to happen.

The New Mini is quite a bit larger than its predecessor. In fact it is larger than the Metro and very close in size to the Austin Morris 11/1300, which was one of the most popular family cars of the 1960s and 1970s. However, this is not really noticeable when driving unless swapping from early Mini to New Mini. The vast majority of cars are larger today and continue to evolve that way; take the aforementioned Golf, for example – the new Mark 5 is considerably larger than the original 1970s Mark 1. There are two main reasons for this. Firstly space must be made available for all the required safety features such as crush zones and airbags; and secondly people are on average larger than they were 30 or 40 years ago. Taking these factors into consideration, comparing the dimensions of the New Mini, which is the small car of today, with those of its ancestor makes interesting reading:

Mini size

Car	Length	Width	Height	Wheelbase
Old Mini	3.05m	1.41m	1.35m	2.04m
11/1300	3.73m	1.53m	1.35m	2.38m
Metro	3.40m	1.55m	1.36m	2.25m
New Mini	3.62m	1.68m	1.41m	2.46m

Chapter **Two**

The New Mini in depth

The New Mini range is made up of five main models: Mini One, Mini One D, Mini Cooper, Mini Cooper S, and Mini Convertible (although in many respects the Convertible is a range in itself, comprising three distinct models). It is a clean, simple, and unfussy design externally, with smooth curves and large wheels. The interior is more retro, but everything is clearly and boldly designed and easy to use. Underneath all this the car is very high tech, with numerous electronic systems and driver and safety aids.

There is actually much more to the New Mini than it would first appear, and in this chapter we will take a look at the various design and engineering features that it incorporates.

The design

The body design of the New Mini is distinctive and sets it apart from every other car on the road. It has cheeky

Side profile of a Mini One D. Some lines follow on from the original design.

Left: A design sketch – this was closer in appearance to the original design ... than the finished product. (Both BMW Press)

Right: Shaping the New Mini – the first clay model. (BMW Press)

Below right: Design of the New Mini is very smooth and the windows give the impression that they surround the car.

yet chunky styling, and above the waistline creates the impression that the car is pillarless. This is because the B and C pillars are hidden behind the side window glass. BMW say this idea has been taken from architecture, where building support structures are sometimes hidden behind glass panels. The rear side windows are bonded, which, apart from improving appearances by removing the need for large rubber seals, contributes to bodyshell stiffness. The lack of vertical body colour between the windows gives the impression that the car is lower than it actually is. The A pillars either side of the front windscreen are disguised by a glass-like black trim panel to maintain the effect, the use of glass not being possible here as the required curvature was impossible to achieve. Tinted glass is fitted as standard to all windows. The doors are fitted with frameless windows, which drop and lift automatically when the door is opened and closed (this is the same system as on the BMW 3 Series Coupé and Convertible models, as well as the Z8). The rear window is heated as standard and the screen washer jet is incorporated in the rear wiper.

Along with the introduction of the Mini Convertible range, from July 2004 all Minis were fitted with new clear glass headlights for brighter illumination. The optional Xenon headlights were also modified to include an additional ring of light spots to increase visibility. Additionally the front and rear bumpers were redesigned on the Mini One and Cooper. The front bumper has been lowered slightly, while at the rear, the rubbing strip has been split, with the fog light repositioned between the two halves (previously the rubbing strip was a single unit with the fog light above). The reversing lights have been integrated into newly designed rear light clusters.

Safety features

One area where the old Mini fell down, particularly in its latter years, was in safety. New cars have to achieve ever escalating safety standards, and this is the major reason for the increase in size of the New Mini compared to the old model, and also to cars in general.

The theme continues at the B post ... and to the rear. Curved glass covers the roof pillars.

The New Mini scores very well when it comes to driver and passenger safety. From the beginning it was designed to reach the NCAP four-star crash test rating, and during the design stage both virtual and real crash tests were carried out. To improve the impact characteristics a lot of work went into engine alignment and engineering the front axle to absorb energy from the floorpan. Further energy-absorbing zones have been designed in to prevent footwell intrusion. This is very reassuring in a small car such as the Mini.

New Mini body stiffness is two to three times greater than that of its competitors. It is one of the stiffest body structures that BMW has produced, with torsional strength equal to that of the current E46 3 Series. All of this is a considerable achievement given the fact that the original 'wheel in each corner' Mini characteristic

has been retained. Stiffness is important in crash protection, as during an impact energy can be absorbed by the crush zones and directed away from the occupants, whilst the body acts as an effective passenger protection shell. A stiff bodyshell brings other benefits too. It contributes to the overall driving experience, improving and sharpening handling and helping with internal acoustics.

All models in the Mini range are fitted with driver and front passenger and side airbags as standard. The front airbags interact with the seat belt latch tensioners and the belt force limiters and inflate according to the severity of an accident. There is also an optional head

Above right: Driver and front passenger side-protection airbags are fitted as standard. (BMW Press)

Right: The crash structure, coupled with the airbags, provides impressive protection for the occupants. (BMW Press)

airbag system, the Advanced Head Protection System (AHPS). The rear seats are fitted with three-point seat belts and adjustable headrests, and Isofix child seat fittings are available as an option.

Another different type of safety feature is the Safety Battery Terminal Clamp (SBC). This interrupts the flow of electricity between the starter and the battery in a severe impact, to help lessen the risk of a fire starting. This is fitted to Mini Cooper S and One D models, where the battery is located in the rear of the car rather than in the engine compartment, in the case of the Cooper S to counterbalance the weight of the supercharger.

Yet another inbuilt safety feature is the Tyre Pressure Warning System, designed to alert the driver to a puncture and possible blowout. Approximately 80 per cent of all blowouts can be detected before the tyre bursts; the tyre pressure warning system is therefore an invaluable safety feature, allowing the driver to react to any loss of tyre pressure in good time. The system monitors the number of times the wheel turns via the sensors in the ABS system and carries out a comparison with the diagonally opposite wheel, comparing the average speeds. A light will illuminate in

Bold door mirrors are along the lines of the BMW M3.

the speedometer display to warn the driver if the pressure is falling in one of the tyres.

Inside the New Mini

Access to the rear seats is very important in any two- or three-door car, and the New Mini is very good in this respect, as its doors open very wide (up to a maximum of 80°). There is also a rather useful front seat tilting mechanism that both tilts and slides the seat forward in one movement; this has a memory function that returns both the backrest and cushion to the starting position when the squab is pushed back. This can take a little mastering, as it is easy to apply insufficient pressure to return the backrest to its correct position, thus leaving the seat angled slightly forward. There is plenty of headroom in the front and it is very reasonable in the rear as well, since the bucket type rear seats create a very low seating position. Rear armrests are integrated in the side trim.

The driver's seat is height adjustable. This is also available as an option for the front passenger's seat. Lumbar support is included with the cloth/leather and full leather seat options. BMWs have always been some of the best drivers' cars in the world and the new Mini is no exception. The driving position is based upon that of the BMW 3 Series, and it is possible for drivers of any shape or size to find a comfortable posture. This is proven by the fact that the seat adjusted to allow my 12-year-old son (who is a member of the Under 17s Car Club) to comfortably drive a New Mini on private land. In all other cars to date he has needed booster cushions.

Instrumentation is bold with a large central speedometer, a design feature taken from the original Mini, which had one central dial when first launched and a grouping of three later on. The central air vents mimic the two additional instruments from the early Cooper and Super De Luxe Mini three-instrument oval binnacle. The New Mini speedometer – which has a silver frame, another link to the past – is fitted with non-reflecting glass and also houses the fuel gauge and water temperature gauge, plus the service interval indicator and LCD mileometer. It is a modern interpretation that works well, being clear and easy to read. The Mini One D, Cooper, and S models are fitted with a rev counter as standard, which is located in front of the driver on the steering column. If the optional navigation system is ordered, the speedo moves next to the rev counter, with the satellite navigation display taking its place in the central dial. The steering wheel is height-adjustable, and on the Cooper models there is a multifunction steering wheel option which enables direct operation of the stereo system and cruise control.

Below the speedometer in the centre console is a bank of up to six chrome plated toggle switches which operate the electric windows, the front and rear fog lights, ASC+T (Automatic Stability Control and Traction) where fitted, and central locking. This is another piece of retro Mini design. The switches seem lower down than on the 1959 design but are closer to the driver, being just in front of the gear lever. Above the toggles the central panel houses the controls for the stereo system, air recirculation, heated rear window, and windscreen blower, plus air conditioning and heated windscreen switches when these options have been specified.

On the floor panel between the driver and front passenger are a lighter, cupholder, and ashtray. To the rear are control switches for the side mirrors, heated

Features such as traction control are standard on some models and optional on the others.

Driver's eye view. The windscreen is quite upright compared to other modern cars, a design feature that was deliberately retained from the old car.

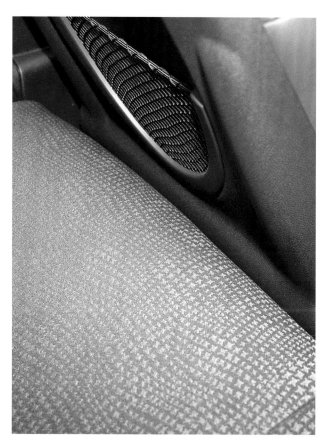

Above: Rear seat legroom is reasonable when the front seats are fairly well forward.

Right: If a very tall driver or passenger is sitting in the front the car is reduced to a 2+2.

Below: Heart of the petrol-engined New Minis – the four-cylinder 1,600cc Pentagon engine.

The engine is chain driven, the system preferred by BMW.

seat switches (when ordered), and the reset button for the tyre pressure indicator. A further cupholder is built into the unit at the back for the use of rear passengers.

It has to be said that boot space is not the New Mini's best feature, but carrying large loads is not what this car is all about. When only two or three people are travelling the rear seat(s) fold forward to an almost horizontal position. The latches to release the seats, which are split 50:50, are accessed from the boot.

New Minis are able to carry a maximum load of 430kg (948lb) and the total loading capacity with seats folded flat is 670 litres. With both rear seats in the upright position there is 150 litres of space.

New Mini electrics

The New Mini's electronics system uses the same wires and cables for different functions, as opposed to the usual one wire per function. The system is split into two circuits. The first connects the engine management, brakes, electronic driver aids, transmission, and instruments; the second is responsible for the vehicle body electrics and electronics, including the interior lights, air conditioning, doors, and electric windows. Integration of the two systems and data transfer between them

offers advantages over conventional electrical systems. The double circuit reduces the number of wires and connectors, making the system very reliable and simplifying assembly.

Remote control central locking to the doors, tailgate, and petrol filler comes as standard on all models and can be operated up to 15m away. The interior light comes on when the central locking is operated. There is a standard key-operated immobiliser, and New Minis made from September 2002 lock automatically at 9mph and unlock when the ignition is turned off. An alarm system is fitted to the Cooper S, and is an optional extra on the Mini One, One D, and Cooper.

The New Mini is fitted with elliptical halogen headlights which feature an unusual reflector system that produces three beams from two bulbs and generates up to 25 per cent more light intensity than the combined power of the two bulbs. The system was further refined in July 2004. Xenon headlights are an option. All Minis come with a radio and cassette player and six speakers (four in the front doors and two in the rear side panels). A number of system upgrade options are available.

Engine and transmission

The engine is mounted transversely and drives the front wheels in true Mini tradition. The engine is not, however, of either BMW or Rover origin but is a Chrysler-built four-cylinder unit known as the Pentagon. Developed by Chrysler and BMW, this was new when first fitted to the New Mini, but the same basic engine design has since been fitted to the Chrysler Neon and PT Cruiser. In the New Mini range it is a smooth and responsive unit in all of its variations. Manufactured in Curitiba, Brazil, the engines are shipped to Plant Oxford, where they are fitted to the gearboxes, followed by the attachment of the remaining ancillaries.

There are plenty of small neat design features, such as the roof mounted clock.

A cutaway view of the compact Mini One/Cooper engine. (BMW Press)

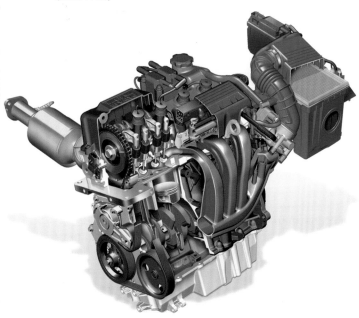

The petrol engines have a cast iron block with a 77mm bore and 85.8mm stroke. The 16-valve aluminium head has an overhead camshaft driven by a maintenance free timing chain (BMW wisely prefer timing chains to cam belts). The engines are exactly the same in the Mini One and the Mini Cooper, the difference in power output – which is 90bhp for the Mini One and 115bhp in the case of the Cooper – being down to electronic control. In the 163bhp Mini Cooper S the basic engine design remains the same but the crankshaft, connecting rods, pistons, engine bearings, and valves have been uprated to cope with the increased thermal and mechanical loads produced by the supercharger. An oil cooler, albeit a very small one, is fitted, and there is splash oil cooling of the pistons to provide additional engine cooling.

All the petrol engines can run on lead free petrol between 91 and 98 octane, meaning that special adjustments do not need to be made for different markets around the world. Engine management is taken care of by a Siemens Powertrain Controller. This controls the throttle by wire technology, which replaces the mechanical cable linkage. When the accelerator is pressed the information is passed to the controller, which increases the fuel supply to the engine. The controller also monitors engine torque: if the required torque is below the maximum potential the controller will retard the ignition timing to provide a rapid pick up, which will be noted by the driver particularly at lower speeds.

BMW have a habit of making regular small but worthwhile engineering improvements to their range and in this respect the Mini is no exception. From July 2004 modifications to the transmission increased engine flexibility in the mid-range, improving torque and acceleration figures.

The Mini One D is fitted with a very economical 75bhp 1,363cc 16-valve turbocharged diesel engine which is described in detail in Chapter 4.

Manual models have a maintenance-free hydraulic clutch. The original manual New Mini gearbox was based on a modified version of an MG Rover box and was manufactured by Midland Gears, a BMW-owned company. Cooper S models are fitted with a six-speed Getrag gearbox, the sixth gear ratio providing a cruising gear to reduce fuel consumption on long journeys – top speed in the S is achieved in fifth gear. The Mini One D also has a six-speed Getrag gearbox but with different ratios, and from July 2004 all Mini One and Mini Cooper models have been fitted with a new five-speed Getrag gearbox with modified gear ratios, resulting in improved acceleration.

The gearchange is smooth, quick, and precise on all New Minis, and the gear lever is connected to the gearbox by means of Bowden cables.

Drive is transmitted to the front wheels by equal length driveshafts, the equal length being achieved by a driveshaft bearing fitted to the engine block. Equal length driveshafts help to eliminate torque steer, which is a common problem in front-wheel drive cars, particularly those with high power outputs. For owners who prefer more relaxed driving, or use their New Mini mainly in towns and cities, automatic transmission is available as an option on Mini One and Cooper models in the form of Continuously Variable Transmission (CVT). More details can be found on this in Chapter 9.

Suspension and steering

One of the New Mini's best features is its phenomenal roadholding capability. The centre of gravity is very low and weight distribution is 63 per cent front and 37 per cent rear. Add to this the long wheelbase and wide track and it is easy to see why the car handles so well. The suspension set-up consists of MacPherson struts at the front, while the rear axle design is based on BMW's patented multi link Z axle fitted to the 3 Series. The Z axle allows the wheels to adjust to the best possible angle in relation to the road, maximising tyre contact under all conditions. The design was modified

Front suspension is MacPherson strut. Vented discs at the front are standard across the range.

to save space, minimise intrusion, and keep the load floor low in the rear of the car. Very successful with rear-wheel drive, this is only the second time that the Z axle has been fitted to a front-wheel drive car (it was first used in this configuration in the Rover 75).

The Cooper has uprated Sports Suspension and sits 8mm lower than the Mini One, while the Cooper S

The New Mini suspension is mounted on subframes, with MacPherson struts at the front and BMW's Z axle at the rear. (BMW Press)

features the further uprated Sports Suspension Plus. All models are fitted with a front anti-roll bar, a reinforced bar being fitted to the Cooper and Cooper S, which also have a rear anti roll-bar.

The New Mini's rack-and-pinion power steering is very responsive and offers excellent feedback through the steering wheel. It requires 2.5 turns from lock to lock. The power element is unusual in that it is 'electrohydraulic' – the hydraulic pump is powered by an electric motor rather than being engine driven. When the steering wheel is turned the pump produces

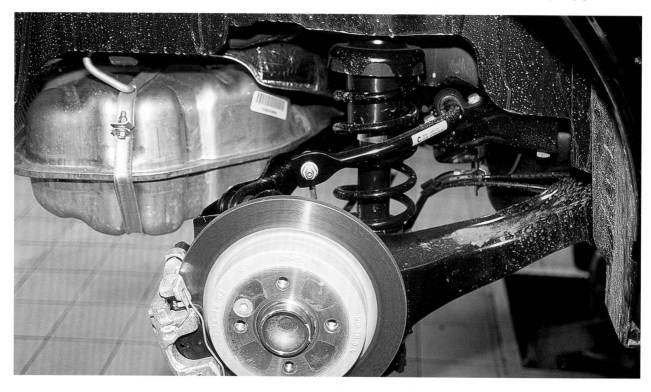

a characteristic whine unique to the New Mini. The Mini One D has an engine driven power steering pump.

Instead of carrying a spare wheel the Mini is equipped with the Mini Mobility System. This consists of a sealant and a compressor that is stored in the boot. In the event of a puncture the tyre pressure warning indicator described above will alert the driver, who must stop and fill the tyre with the sealant, which is put in through the valve. Tyre pressure can then be restored using the compressor. Sixteen-inch run-flat tyres are supplied with the Mini Cooper S. These have reinforced side walls and are made from heat-resistant rubber. Functions such as ABS, ASC+T or DSC (Dynamic Stability Control) are not affected if pressure is lost, and the driver can continue the journey for up to 80 miles at speeds of up to 50 mph. Even if fully deflated, the tyres can safely run at 30mph.

Run-flat tyres are only available on 16in wheels and are an option on the Mini One, Mini One D, and Mini Cooper.

Brakes

All New Mini models have diagonal dual circuit brakes, with disc brakes all round. The front discs are 276mm x 22mm and are ventilated; the rears are solid and are 259mm x 10mm. The braking system includes the BMW Group standard electronic brake control and stability systems, four sensor ABS (Anti Lock Braking System),

Electronic Braking Distribution (EBD), and Cornering Brake Control (CBC).

EBD controls the braking force between the front and rear wheels to ensure correct braking power distribution under different loads and conditions. It is activated under average braking pressures, a long time before ABS would normally kick in. Unlike ABS, EBD is not detectable by and cannot be deactivated by the driver.

CBC prevents the car from becoming unstable when braking through corners. The electronic system detects side slip of the wheels via the ABS sensors if the car becomes unstable. This can occur if the brakes are applied heavily while cornering. The system recognises that the car is cornering and feeds more braking force to the outside front wheel when necessary, thereby reducing the possibility of sliding or skidding.

Plant Oxford

Production of the New Mini was originally to have taken place at Longbridge, but the breaking up of the Rover Group and the retention by BMW of the Mini and the factory at Cowley meant that the newly built production facilities had to be moved to the latter from Longbridge.

New Mini production began at Oxford in April 2001,

The electrohydraulic power steering pump.

The Cooper S, the most eagerly awaited new car for a very long time.

42 years after the first Morris Mini Minor came off the line at the same factory – a fact that BMW likes to promote. The factory employs a workforce of around 4,500, the success of the New Mini having led to the creation of over 700 new jobs since its launch in July 2001. New Minis are all built to order. Well over 100,000 cars are built each year, which means 500 are made every day. To meet with this world-wide demand the plant currently works seven days a week on a

three-shift system – an early and late shift Monday to Thursday plus a permanent weekend shift.

The bodyshell is produced in a virtually fully-automated production process that features 230 industrial robots. Once the body is built it goes to the paintshop. A New Mini takes ten hours to paint in a seven-stage process that also applies protective coatings and water-based varnishes. The paint shop is in the unique position of finishing two of its four models with a black or white contrasting roof.

The completed white bodyshell is cleaned to remove

DID YOU KNOW?

The New Mini paintshop has over 10km of paint circulation pipes and 14km of conveyors.

body is coated with a two pack clear coat. The finish on the New Mini range is excellent, particularly so for a car within this price range. In the words of *Autocar* in their first test of the Mini One, 'No £10k car has ever had paint this glossy'.

Once the painting process is complete it moves to the final assembly line to be fitted with the 2,415 different parts that make up each New Mini. Although a German-owned company, BMW say that UK suppliers account for 40 per cent of the purchased material value.

The New Mini market

Mini is an independent brand within the BMW Group and is available in over 70 markets world-wide, ranging from China to Mexico. In the UK the New Mini is sold from a network of 148 dedicated dealerships which are either stand-alone or else form part of an existing BMW dealership, in which case they are in a separate part of the building. At the time of writing the UK had six stand-alone Mini dealerships, but BMW say that this number will increase as the brand continues to gain strength. Mini sales staff are dedicated to selling New Minis rather than both Minis and BMWs. However, there is a notable enthusiasm for Mini among the staff on the BMW side as well.

By June 2003 Plant Oxford had manufactured over 250,000 New Minis for world-wide distribution since production began in 2001. Seventy-five per cent of all New Mini production is exported, with the UK being the largest market, followed by the USA and then Germany.

Who buys a New Mini? The overall answer to this is all types of people, young and old, male or female, single or married, celebrity or factory worker. There is no typical owner. However, BMW's main target market is young people aged between 20 and 34 with reasonable disposable income. These will buy a New Mini as their main car. The secondary target market is people aged between 35 and 50, who in many cases will have owned an original Mini. In this group the New Mini will be the second or third car. UK buyers are of all ages and social backgrounds, spread evenly throughout the country, and split 50:50 between the sexes.

any unwanted particles that are present following the assembly and welding. Once clean, the entire body is dipped and zinc phosphate coated, after which the first priming coat of paint is applied by means of cathodic electrodeposition, which is the basis for permanent protection against corrosion. The body is then coated with a surfacer primer, after which it is cleaned again by a mechanical duster which, amazingly, is made of ostrich feathers. Presumably this is to ensure complete cleanliness 'down under' as well as on top.

The colour top coat is applied next, after which the

The Mini One

The Mini One is the entry level New Mini. It is BMW's basic version of the Mini Range. In the case of most cars, both past and present, an entry level car is by its very nature somewhat poorly equipped in order to keep

The Mini One. This press car is fitted with a number of extras to make it stand out.

the price as low as possible, and therefore usually commands little attention. Normally it will have the smallest engine, least attractive trim, and be bought by the driver who wants a utilitarian vehicle as a means of transport and little else. Often base models do not get looked after very well and mechanical and body condition alike suffer after just a few years.

The Mini One is a complete exception to this, for a number of reasons. First and foremost it is a Mini, and the Mini commands great affection. Most people who buy Minis love them, and as a result they usually look after them. To prove this point is not difficult. The Mini is still a new car, and there hasn't been sufficient time for them to become battered and scruffy; but even taking this into account it is rare to see a dirty or neglected New Mini. Their owners take pride in them.

The build quality of the Mini One is, as with all Minis, very high – one of the advantages of a car built by a prestige manufacturer. BMW quality shows through. The bodywork fit and finish is outstanding, the panel gaps are even, and the paint quality is probably higher than on not just any other car in its own market sector but on most of those above.

The Mini One is an important model in the New Mini range. It is attractively trimmed and presented both externally and internally and, what is more, it comes with a very reasonable level of standard equipment, and an even larger range of optional extras.

One neat and clear rear badge.

Considering the standard equipment and what is possible with the car it is also attractively priced. At the time of writing the Mini One was just under 12½ per cent cheaper than the Mini Cooper at UK prices.

Right from the beginning the Mini One received good reports from the press, particularly as it was being

It may be the entry-level car, but it's One to keep up with. (BMW Press)

Rear view of the One.

weighed up, in price versus performance and equipment levels, against the Mini Cooper. All those who road tested the car liked it, and the level of

Below: Standard road wheels on the One are steel with plastic hub caps.

Below right: The car featured was fitted with optional alloys as is the case with many Mini Ones.

affection felt for the Mini One was well summed up by *Autocar* in their first road test in July 2001, when they said: 'We can't think of a car that has nailed mass instant desirability with the weight and precision of the new Mini, and that applies as much to the entry level Mini One as to the Cooper.' Praise indeed. How often does a base model achieve this?

Perhaps one of the main appeals of the Mini One is that at first sight it doesn't really look all that different from the Cooper, and there can be little doubt that the

The One interior. Upholstery is snazzy, seats are comfortable.

The rear seating area of the One.

untrained eye will not be able spot the difference between models. But then this is something that Mini has always been about: the original 1960s Coopers were only distinguished by grilles, badges, and a chrome trim around the tops of the doors, and only the enthusiast really knew which was which unless the car was stationary so that the badge could be read.

In standard form the Mini One is monotone. This looks good and in theory distinguishes it from the other models in the range (with the exception of its sister car, the Mini One D). However, to add confusion some Cooper and S owners order their cars in monotone, while some Mini One owners can't resist the temptation of a white roof. Other more definite distinguishing features of the standard Mini One are

DID YOU KNOW?

Despite some similarity in appearance there are actually no common parts in the new and old Minis. The badges look very similar, but a close comparison will reveal that even these are a slightly different shape.

The classic design of dashboard.

the black radiator grille centre and the black vinyl finish door mirrors. Completely standard Mini Ones are equipped with 5.5 x 15 steel wheels fitted with silver finished plastic hubcaps and 175/65R15 tyres, but, certainly in the UK and in many other countries too, the majority of Mini Ones are actually fitted with optional alloy wheels. Fitting alloys upmarkets the overall appearance of the car considerably.

Many owners further dress their Mini One either to individualise it or to resemble the Mini Cooper more closely. This is very easily achieved and is ideal for younger drivers – or anyone else for that matter – who seek to create the look and prestige of owning a Cooper without the problems of an increased insurance premium. Details of many of the options and accessories available from BMW are to be found in Chapter 9.

Inside the Mini One has the same bold layout as all New Minis. The seats are trimmed with Aqua cloth fabric; the steering wheel adjusts for both rake and height; and the seats are comfortable. Everyone should be able to find their ideal driving position, particularly as the driver's seat is height adjustable, though there is no lumbar support adjustment unless the optional leather upholstery is specified. The Mini One is likely to be a second car option for many, but it is well up to the job of first car for single people or small families – the

fact that rear legroom and boot space is very limited rules it out as a main family car unless the children are very young. The rear seats split 50:50, a feature which is sometimes missing from entry level cars, and this is very useful for carrying larger items.

Standard equipment includes the service interval indicator and tyre pressure indicator, and, as with all Minis, four airbags, four disc brakes, Electronic Brake force Distribution, and Cornering Brake Control.

Engine, gearbox, and running gear

The Mini One's 1,598cc engine is exactly the same as that fitted in the Cooper model and is described in the previous chapter, but the power output is reduced by the engine electronics to 90bhp. With 103lb/ft at 3,000rpm it pulls well and is a very flexible unit.

The suspension is well damped. The main differences between the set-up on the Mini One and Cooper models are in the stiffness of the front anti-roll bar, and the fact that an anti roll bar is not fitted to the rear. The Mini One rides 8mm higher than the Cooper, and the suspension is also noticeably softer than the Sports Suspension of the latter. This has the advantage of giving a more comfortable ride, especially over rutted roads and speed bumps, yet somehow the handling still manages to remain pin sharp, with cornering ability second to very little. The conventional MacPherson struts at the front work well with the BMW Z axle at the rear to give a well balanced, drivable, fun car.

On the road

The Mini One is immense fun to drive. Its 'Mininess' shines through and encourages spirited driving. It is one of those rare cars capable of making the journey to work something to look forward to just as much as the journey home. The softer suspension does result in some increased body roll through fast bends and corners when compared to models further up the New Mini range, but this is not a problem, especially when taking the lower power output of the engine into account. Take the Mini One onto a race track, though, and the roll is a lot more noticeable and, correspondingly, tyre grip is lost sooner, but we're talking here of pushing the car to the limit; even with very fast driving on the road this will not be a problem.

The steering rack is quick and responsive and even in its lowest powered petrol form the New Mini just cries out to be seriously driven rather than pottered around. This fun element – the go-kart handling and ultra-sharp steering response – recreates the experience enjoyed by owners of the original Mini. Regular drivers of the old Mini often thought the

steering sloppy in other cars, particularly rear-wheel drive cars, and the fact that the New Mini, even at entry level, can do the same today (although perhaps to a lesser extent, due to improvements in other cars) is a credit to the engineers who created it.

Some New Mini drivers actually prefer the One to the Cooper. It is every bit as enjoyable and as fun to drive as the rest of the range, even though it may not be as fast – in a Mini speed is not everything, and in a lower powered car it is easier to use the full potential. Driving a pre-production press Mini One over hilly winding roads through the Brecon Beacons in Wales showed off the car's capabilities well. Performance was good, and acceleration reasonably brisk, as it should be in a car

One at speed, capably overtaking the opposition. (BMW Press)

with a 0–60 time of 10.9 seconds. The only time the lower power in this pre-production model really showed was when overtaking a lorry uphill; however, since the production press car seemed to have more power this could probably be put down simply to the newness of this early example.

The Mini One will turn just as many heads as the Cooper models too. With its Liquid Yellow paint finish and bold black Viper Stripes, the Mini One featured in this chapter – which was on test from the Mini press fleet – attracted more attention and favourable comment from passers by than the Cooper S or even the Cooper S Works!

MINI ONE STANDARD EQUIPMENT

Anti-lock Brake System (ABS)
Cornering Brake Control (CBC)
Crash Sensor
Disc brakes all round, ventilated at front
Electronic Braking Distribution (EBD)
Mini Mobility System
Tyre Defect Indicator
Two front and two side airbags
Three-point safety belts with pre-tensioners and belt force
    limiters
15in steel wheels with hubcaps
Colour-coded front and rear bumpers
Chrome door handles
Electric door mirrors in matt black
Third brake light
Tinted glass
50:50-split folding rear seats
Aqua cloth upholstery
Front and rear cupholders
Digital clock
Easy entry function
Frameless electric front windows
Electro Hydraulic power steering
Height adjustable driver's seat
Height adjustable steering wheel
Thatcham CAT2 immobiliser
Radio cassette with six speakers
Remote central locking
Rev counter (from July 2004)

Chapter **Four**

The Mini
One D

The Mini One D was the fourth model to be introduced into the New Mini range. What makes it particularly special is that it is the first model in the history of the Mini to be fitted with a diesel engine. As a point of interest for students of Mini history, BMC did produce a 1-litre diesel A Series engine, but this was fitted to a tractor – it never made it into the original Mini, as there would have been no demand for a diesel-engined small car in the 1960s and 1970s. Things are very different in the 21st century, and sales of diesel cars in the UK are continually rising; they did so for 30 consecutive months prior to the introduction of the Mini One D in June 2003 and will account for 30 per cent of new car sales in 2004. In Europe diesel sales have always been very strong.

Visually the Mini One D is virtually identical to the petrol-engined Mini One. Minor differences include a 'D' badge at the rear, Mini Cooper S sills, larger air

The Mini One D. The different Cooper S-style sills can be clearly seen.

This press car is more subtle than the petrol engined One press car.

intakes for the intercooler in the front panel, and the exhaust tailpipe hidden by the rear valence. Inside the trim and dashboard is the same as the Mini One, but the One D is fitted with a rev counter as standard, which also incorporates the external temperature display. An electronic immobiliser (Thatcham category grade two), activated from the key via a transponder, is standard. Like the Mini One, four airbags, four disc brakes, EBD, and CBC come in the package.

The diesel engine

The heart of the Mini One D is a four-cylinder turbocharged and intercooled 1,364cc direct-injection diesel engine with second generation common rail

Above: Except for the standard fitment rev counter the interior is the same as the petrol-driven One.

Right: Rear boot space is limited on all models.

Below right: With the seat down space is increased for carrying larger loads. The One D is probably the Mini which will receive the most utility use.

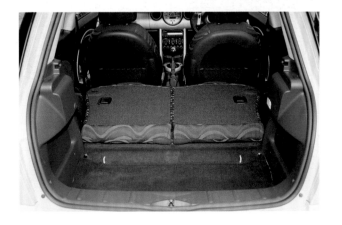

technology. Like all Mini engines this is not of BMW origin but is imported, being the Toyota 1ND-TV unit used in the Yaris. However, like the petrol engines it has been further developed by the BMW Group.

This engine develops 75bhp at 4,000rpm and the maximum torque of 133lb/ft is developed at just 2,000rpm. It is able to build up two-thirds of its maximum torque at 1,500rpm, which means that the fun element constituting a lot of what the New Mini is all about is still very much present. High torque at low revs, though, is typical of a diesel engine and makes the Mini One D an ideal city car. It is very suitable for long runs too, its fuel economy being excellent: the combined cycle fuel consumption figure is 58.9mpg, which BMW point out means that, depending on individual driving style, the Mini One D is able to travel in excess of 600 miles on

Left: Diesel heart. The Toyota-derived Mini One D engine.

Below left: A D after the 'ONE' badge denotes that this is an oil burning Mini.

Bottom left: Apart from the badge, the give-away that this is a diesel is the tailpipe.

a full tank of fuel – the equivalent of driving the entire length of Britain from the Isle of Skye to the Isle of Wight. The official urban consumption figure is 48.7mpg, and in extra urban conditions 65.7mpg.

These figures mean that the Mini One D fares very well against the competition, and make it the most fuel efficient production car to be built by the BMW group.

Even with good fuel consumption there is no performance penalty. Top speed is 103mph, 0–62mph acceleration time is 13.8 seconds, and accelerating from 50–75mph in fourth gear takes 12.3 seconds.

The One D is every bit as fun as the petrol version. The S side sills stand out in this photograph. (BMW Press)

All are very reasonable figures for a small diesel-
engined car, and when driving it feels quicker than
they suggest.

The engine has bore of 73mm and stroke of 81.5mm.
The engine block and cylinder head are made of
aluminium, which helps keep the weight of the Mini
One D down to 1,175kg, compared to 1,140kg for the
Mini One. It uses lightweight pistons that run in liners
made of grey cast iron. There are four valves per
cylinder and an overhead camshaft. The compression
ratio 18.5:1.

The camshaft is driven by the crankshaft via a
maintenance-free timing chain: as with the New Mini
petrol engines, BMW are steering clear of a cam belt.

A different look, and a different sound, but the engine is surprisingly
quiet for a small four-cylinder diesel.

Two independent poly-V-belts drive the ancillaries, such
as the alternator, water pump, and air conditioning
compressor, as well as the servo pump on the hydraulic
power steering (the electro hydraulic steering fitted to
the petrol-engined model is not fitted to the One D).
There is a damper at the front end of the crankshaft
which absorbs the diesel engine vibrations, to minimise
transmission of these to the drive belts.

The second generation common rail diesel
technology is one of BMW's modifications to the
Toyota engine. It incorporates intelligent computer-
controlled Bosch fuel injection to supply fuel at exactly
the right time and under extremely high pressure
directly into the combustion chambers. The common
rail which acts as a pressure reservoir supplies fuel to
the injection jets and a pump makes sure that the fuel
in the pressure reservoir remains under high pressure
at up to 1,600 bar. The first generation original Toyota
system was only 1,350 bar, and the increase boosts the
peak torque figure by 7lb/ft. The high pressure assists
atomisation of the fuel into extremely fine particles,
resulting in quieter, cleaner, and more efficient
combustion. Electronic engine management controls

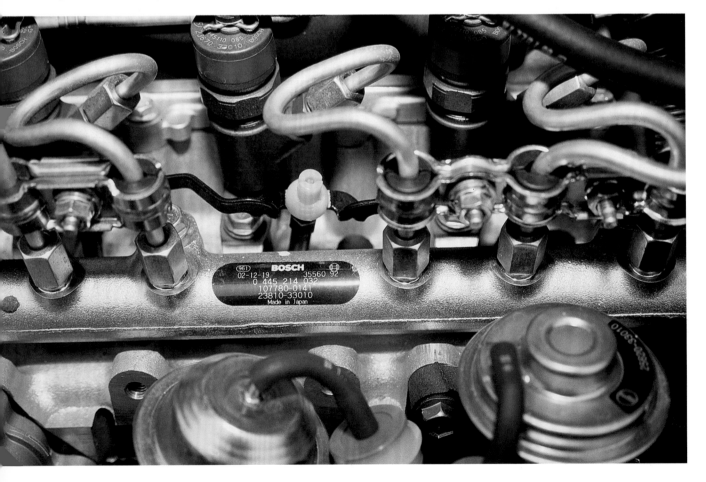

the timing and duration of both the pilot and main injection processes. The pilot injection feeds a small amount of fuel into the combustion chambers prior to the main injection; as a result the fuel/air mix burns more smoothly than with a conventional set-up. The smoother rise of pressure in the combustion chambers also helps to keep the combustion process noise down to a minimum, and also sees a reduction in emissions. This is a very clean diesel. It can run on sulphur-free fuel, which further reduces soot particle formation. The oxidation catalytic converter which is built into the exhaust system means that the One D out-performs the EU 3 emission standard. Like the petrol-engined cars, the Mini One D has a wire-free throttle.

The turbocharger compressor runs at speeds of up to 225,000rpm and compresses the fresh air to an overpressure of 1.2 bar. To overcome the resulting heat problem the air is cooled by an intercooler before it reaches the combustion chamber. The One D intercooler is fitted next to the engine radiator and receives its supply of air through the radiator grille.

Of course, diesel engines can be a problem to start in cold weather, but not so the One D. It is fitted with a quick start pre-heater system which is very effective and certainly worked well on the car featured in this chapter, which was tested in some of Britain's coldest weather. To combat the problem of small diesels not providing very good heating for the car's occupants, the One D features an additional electrical heater.

The service interval on the One D is 15,000 miles, 5,000 more than with the petrol models. This is achieved by the use of high performance oil and an oil level sensor that consistently monitors the amount of oil in the sump. There is also an oil/water heat exchanger that maintains correct temperatures and helps prevent the engine oil from ageing prematurely.

Transmission is the six-speed Getrag gearbox from the Mini Cooper S, with the gear ratios altered to match the diesel's flatter torque curve. First gear is lower and the other five are higher, with sixth gear effectively being an overdrive for economical and relaxed cruising.

DID YOU KNOW?

BMW have a Performance Centre at Rockingham in Corby, Northamptonshire. The Centre offers visitors test drives and high performance training, and children aged 12 to 16 can have their first driving experience on the roads around the circuit in a Mini One D.

Another optional alloy style that is available on the One models.

A dual mass flywheel in the transmission prevents engine vibrations being transmitted to the cabin, especially at low revs.

Running gear

The One D weighs in at only 35kg more than the Mini One, and consequently there are no modifications to the suspension or brakes. The only difference in this department is that because of the high torque being produced at low revs ASC+T is fitted as standard to prevent wheelspin on slippery surfaces. The Mini One D is fitted with the same 15in steel wheels and 175 section tyres as its petrol-engined counterpart.

On the road

The Mini One D is the ideal car for the high mileage Mini driver, as it provides excellent economy without losing any of the fun elements and driving enjoyment that are what the New Mini is all about. On the road the suspension felt firmer on the car featured here than it did on the petrol-engined Mini One, a fact also commented on by rear seat passengers. The engine is detectable as a diesel when it is first fired up, and it feels as if it makes very slightly more noise than the petrol cars when running at motorway speeds. This is not to say that the One D is a noisy car, it isn't at all; it is maybe just a tad noisier than the petrol car. In fact from inside the cabin it is almost impossible to distinguish whether the car is petrol or diesel above idle speeds.

Rear view of the One D. This car is fitted with optional 8-spoke 15in alloy wheels. (BMW Press)

The engine is very torquey, which makes the One D very drivable and every bit as much fun as the One or Cooper. Some people say that it is actually preferable to the Cooper, but this is really a matter of personal preference. The One D is a great car with great performance and excellent fuel consumption, and some owners spec them up with Sports Suspension and alloys and end up with a car which in the end is close to a diesel Cooper.

MINI ONE D STANDARD EQUIPMENT

Anti-lock Brake System (ABS)
Cornering Brake Control (CBC)
Crash Sensor
Disc brakes all round, ventilated at front
Electronic Braking Distribution (EBD)
Mini Mobility System
Tyre Defect Indicator
Two front and two side airbags
Three-point safety belts with pre-tensioners and belt force
    limiters
15in steel wheels with hubcaps
Colour-coded front and rear bumpers
Chrome door handles
Electric door mirrors in matt black
Third brake light
Tinted glass
50:50-split folding rear seats
Aqua cloth upholstery
Front and rear cupholders

Digital clock
Easy entry function
Frameless electric front windows
Electro Hydraulic power steering
Height adjustable driver's seat
Height adjustable steering wheel
Thatcham CAT2 immobiliser
Radio cassette with six speakers
Remote central locking
130A alternator
Six-speed manual gearbox
ASC+T
Exhaust pipe hidden behind rear bumper
Mini Cooper S side sills
Mini One D badging
Rev counter with outside temperature display
Front bumper with larger air inlet
Rev counter (from July 2004)

Chapter **Five**

The Mini Cooper

A new Mini range would never have been complete without some upgraded performance versions – this, after all, is a lot of what the Mini scene is all about. Rather than producing an M Power version of the Mini along the lines of the BMW M3 or M5, BMW wisely decided that they would stick with Mini tradition and use the Cooper name. There would have been nothing wrong with an M Mini, but going the Cooper route not only helped to reinforce the sales and marketing of the Mini as a separate brand to BMW but also pleased Mini enthusiasts and followers the world over.

And the new Mini Cooper is very much a 'proper'

The Mini Cooper, best selling model in the range.

The Cooper looks good in light colours which accentuate the crisp lines.

Cooper, not just a product under licence or a badge-engineered version of the standard car with a couple of go faster stripes. John Cooper, the man who created the original Mini Cooper, and his son Mike were involved from the very beginning with the design and development of the new model. This was intentional on BMW's part, Bernd Pischetsrieder – BMW's top man at the time of the company's acquisition of Rover – having gone out of his way to arrange it.

Frank Stephenson, the leader of the New Mini design team, made a number of visits to John Cooper Garages in East Preston and Ferring to work out what specification upgrades would be required to create Mini Cooper and Cooper S models that would live up to the world's expectations. This cannot have been an easy task bearing in mind both the history of Cooper

DID YOU KNOW?

Brand new Minis are taken from Oxford to the distribution centre by train. This saves over half a million car transporter miles each year.

and the requirements of a performance version of a modern hatchback.

The Rover group, meanwhile, had been going through turbulent times, and matters came to a head with BMW's decision to dispense with it. John Cooper, not surprisingly, was upset by the split, but was pleased that the New Mini would still go ahead. He was also gratified that the new Cooper and Cooper S models would continue the name into the 21st century, and that they would be made at the Cowley factory rather than production being moved elsewhere or even abroad. He was delighted, too, with the way that the New Mini performed, and that the spirit of the old car had been kept alive in the new one. He had good reason to be impressed, for the new Mini Cooper was the most powerful to date: with 115bhp, it delivered 60bhp more than the standard original 997/8.

Sadly John Cooper died on 24 December 2000, having lived to see the new car announced to the public but not long enough to see it launched. Thankfully Cooper involvement didn't end with John's passing but continued under the guidance of his son

Right: Redesigning the Cooper, these are design sketches for the 2004 facelift. (BMW Press)

Dark colours look good too, as can be seen from this Cooper, even though the photos were taken on a dull day.

Mike. This was very much with John's blessing – he had said himself that he felt he 'was' the old Mini and that Mike 'is' the New Mini.

The Mini Cooper is the best selling model in the entire New Mini range. This is not really surprising as (grouping the Cabriolet models together as one) it is placed mid-range in price and performance and is the ideal all-round compromise between the entry model Mini One and the Cooper S. It also sells well because it

carries the Cooper name. Cooper remains one of the best-known names in automotive circles, and although informing someone that you are the owner of a New Mini will command a considerable amount of interest and even respect among those who have little or no interest in cars, adding the word Cooper to the equation adds a significant amount of additional street cred.

The Mini Cooper is an ideal everyday Mini. The performance hike over the One makes it just that bit more capable on long runs, and it is quite a bit more relaxing to drive than the Cooper S, particularly in urban situations. It has a good performance, with 25bhp more than the One. However, it is better classified as a 'warm' hatch rather than a hot hatch – reasonable as its capabilities may be, it doesn't set the tarmac alight, and it is necessary to buy a Cooper S to move into serious hot hatch territory. The Cooper is nevertheless 1.4 seconds faster than the One from 0–60mph, and 10mph faster.

As well as the advantages of its increased performance levels, there are a number of benefits equipment-wise too. The most noticeable of these is the fitting of alloy wheels as standard equipment. From the front, the easiest way to distinguish the Mini Cooper from other models is by its chrome-plated front radiator grille and, below it, the stainless steel mesh lower grille. Then there's the white or black roof which

Another alloy option on the Cooper.

comes as standard – although, to confuse matters, some owners specify their cars in monotone. Such different coloured roofs have always been very much a Cooper distinction; they date right back to 1961 and the very first 997 Cooper, and remained a feature until 1970. Heritage is a big part of the New Mini. Depending

The Mini Cooper at its best, powering along on the open road. (BMW Press)

Above: The Cooper interior layout is basically the same as the Mini One and One D.

Above right: Sports seats are very comfortable.

on roof colour, the Cooper also has white or painted black, rather than black plastic, wing mirrors.

The interior is trimmed in Kaleido cloth. A rev counter is fitted just in front of the driver as standard, and the speedometer remains in the central position. In all other respects the equipment and trim levels are as per the Mini One except for the addition of footwell lights which upmarket the look of the interior at night when the doors are opened. As with other New Minis, the BMW hallmark standard safety equipment is all there: four airbags, four disc brakes, EBD, and CBC.

DID YOU KNOW?

More than one in every 50 new cars sold in the UK in July 2003 was a New Mini.

Engine and gearbox

The Cooper engine is actually exactly the same unit as fitted to the Mini One but with the benefit of an additional 25bhp. The extra performance to justify the Cooper name has been obtained by upgrading the electronic engine management system rather than by the fitting of any uprated or tuned mechanical components. The 0–62 time is reduced to 9.2 seconds and top speed is up to 124mph. Both of these figures can be considered reasonable for a 1,600cc normally aspirated engine and for a car in this class. Performance is brisk rather than quick, and fuel economy remains good, with a combined figure of 41.5mpg.

Transmission-wise there are no changes from the One, the gearbox being the same Rover-derived unit. Mini Coopers made from July 2004 have a five-speed version of the Cooper S Getrag gearbox fitted to the Mini One D and Cooper S. The Rover box is certainly not a bad gearbox, but the Getrag is a definite improvement with a slightly slicker gearchange. There

is also a resulting slight improvement in performance figures.

Running gear

Sports Suspension is fitted as standard. As a result the Cooper sits 8mm lower than the One and One D, which is sufficient to make quite a bit of difference to the handling, particularly in reducing the amount of body

The Mini range is already helping BMW to comply with overall emission targets. Development work is under way towards zero emissions. (BMW Press)

roll. It also improves the appearance of the Cooper slightly – all Minis, old and new, look more aggressive

Heart of the Mini Cooper, the 115bhp engine.

The Cooper retains the petrol filler flap of the less powerful cars.

through the bends than the One. The steering is the same as the One, with pin sharp response, and the excellent four-wheel disc brakes are shared with the rest of the range.

On the road

The Mini Cooper was the first New Mini I drove – through the streets of Cardiff on a Saturday evening at a BMW press launch. Within moments I felt at home. Somehow all of the New Minis are that sort of car: there is a friendly feeling, and the instrumentation and controls can be mastered very quickly thanks to the bold and clear layout.

The Cooper offers very reasonable performance, enough to make it fun. The Mini One is fun as well, of course, but the extra performance of the Cooper definitely gives it an edge when pulling away, and is particularly noticeable and useful when overtaking. It pulls away with good traction and there does not seem to be any torque steer from the 115bhp engine – BMW's equal length driveshafts seem to do the trick. It could be argued on this point that the engine is not powerful enough to make torque steer a problem, but there are other, lower-powered, front-wheel drive cars which do suffer from the problem, and it could even be experienced on a hard-driven standard original 39bhp Mini 1000.

Traction control is not fitted as standard on the Cooper. It can be specified as an option, but it's not

when they sit slightly closer to the road. The anti-roll bar at the front end is stiffer than that fitted to the One and One D, and there is also a rear anti-roll bar, these two items further contributing to the lower level of roll in corners. The improvement is even more noticeable on the track, where the Cooper is considerably quicker

MINI COOPER STANDARD EQUIPMENT

Anti-lock Brake System (ABS)
Cornering Brake Control (CBC)
Crash Sensor
Disc brakes all round, ventilated at front
Electronic Braking Distribution (EBD)
Mini Mobility System
Tyre Defect Indicator
Two front and two side airbags
Three-point safety belts with pre-tensioners and belt force
    limiters
Colour-coded front and rear bumpers
Chrome door handles
Electric door mirrors in matt black
Third brake light
Tinted glass
50:50 split folding rear seats
Kaleido cloth upholstery

Front and rear cupholders
Digital clock
Easy entry function
Frameless electric front windows
Electro hydraulic power steering
Height adjustable driver's seat
Height adjustable steering wheel
Thatcham CAT2 immobiliser
Radio cassette with six speakers
Remote central locking
15in alloy wheels
Chrome grille, tailpipe, and boot handle
Footwell lights
Rev counter
Sports Suspension
Stainless steel mesh grille
White or black roof and wing mirrors

anything like as necessary as it is on the Cooper S – you have to try for wheelspin in the Cooper as opposed to trying not to in the S. The handling is good, the benefits of the Sports Suspension being noticeable, particularly with the extra 25bhp on tap. The ride does suffer slightly, but it is still a perfectly

The silver Cooper photographed for this chapter was loaded with extras such as satellite navigation and a sliding sunroof.

comfortable car to ride in and to drive. The brakes are excellent and will pull the car up reassuringly well.

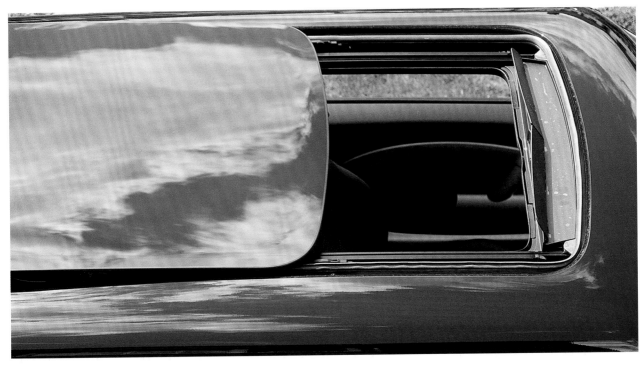

Chapter Six

The Cooper S

The Mini Cooper S was without doubt the New Mini for which everyone had been desperately waiting. BMW have produced outstanding high performance cars for many years, and in the Mini's previous incarnation it was the Cooper S that won most of the races and rallies and made Mini a household name. Add the two

The Mini Cooper S. Subtle changes make it look more aggressive than the lesser powered Cooper.

together, and the arrival of a new S made a very exciting prospect indeed.

Though, with its 1,600cc naturally aspirated engine, the Mini Cooper provided sufficient performance to make it fun to drive, press and motoring enthusiasts alike were really looking for a serious performance model. It had been known for a long time that the S was to be fitted with a supercharged rather than turbocharged engine, and stories had abounded about

pre-production test cars disappearing with lightning acceleration to prevent would-be spies getting a sneak preview. So expectations were high, and when the Cooper S was launched in the UK on 8 June 2002 it certainly did not disappoint. Press reaction was amazing, *Autocar* describing the S as 'the most complete hot hatch ever' and awarding it nine out of ten on their points scale. The only real criticisms levelled by most testers regarded rear legroom and boot space – the same as for the rest of the New Mini range, and not really a major issue on this type of car. The performance and handling received nothing but praise.

The S is the top of the range New Mini, and a number of distinguishing features make it stand out as such. The most immediately noticeable difference is the bonnet scoop, which is not just a styling feature but is necessary to accommodate the air intake scoop which

directs cool air under the bonnet and over the intercooler. The S bonnet consequently sits 40mm higher than those of the standard Mini and Cooper. The bumpers are colour coded as per the rest of the range

The Cooper S's purposeful look is most noticeable at the front end, where the redesigned bumper and body-coloured grille set it apart.

COOPER S

Above left: Cooper S design ideas. (BMW Press)

Left: The wide arches look awesome. (BMW Press)

Above: The biggest telltale that distinguishes a Cooper S is its bonnet air scoop.

Right: The Cooper S badge on the tailgate.

but are of a slightly different design to assist engine cooling and air flow, with a black honeycomb grille in the front bumper through which air is channelled into the engine compartment.

At the rear there are two chrome-plated exhaust tailpipes in the middle of the bumper, below a black honeycomb grille. Along the side the sills are of a more aerodynamic design, and there are two S badged, chrome-plated side grilles with white side indicator repeaters. A large retro styled chrome-plated fuel tank filler cap also loudly shouts Cooper S.

The roof and electric wing mirrors are finished in either white or black. A body-coloured roof with black exterior mirrors is a no-cost option. 6.5 x 16 X-lite alloy wheels with 195/55R16V tyres are fitted as standard, alloy wheels finished in white as opposed to silver

Above: The rear view is also distinctive, the most noticeable feature being the twin tailpipes.

Left: Close-up of the twin tailpipes.

Above right: Side treatment is more subtle, with S badges on the grilles.

Above far right: Six speeds indicate that this is an S.

Right: Inside, the cockpit is much the same as the rest of the range.

being an option for Minis with a white roof. The S also has a roof spoiler in the roof colour, designed to increase downforce on the rear of the car and improve stability at high speeds.

The instrument panel, dashboard, and door frames are finished in brushed aluminium-look plastic, which is designed to complement the Anthracite or Magnesium Grey door trim. Black leather armrests are fitted into the door frames. Two-tone cloth sports seats with a Silver Grey centre and Black Panther side pads come as standard. The height-adjustable sports seats provide a lot more side support during cornering, and, as with the other models in the New Mini range, it is

The S has racier foot pedals and a foot rest.

easy to find an ideal driving position. Many Cooper S models are fitted with optional leather upholstery which includes lumbar support on the front seats: the choices include two 'Satellite' cloth/leather combinations and two 'Gravity' full leather upholstery designs, both in Lapis Blue/Black Panther or Black

Heart of the S, the supercharged 163bhp engine.

Panther/Black Panther and black or blue carpets. Anthracite or Magnesium Grey door trims are available with all five seat trim options. Other goodies fitted as standard include a leather steering wheel, a stainless steel foot-rest to the left of the clutch pedal, and a leather and chrome gearknob.

Like all New Minis, the S comes with plenty of safety equipment built in. This is particularly reassuring on a high performance car. Four airbags, four disc brakes, ABS, EBD, CBC, plus ASC+T, all come as standard kit. Because an S is also likely to be an attractive proposition for thieves there is a an electronic immobiliser and Thatcham approved Category 1 alarm. The alarm system has its own power supply and will set off in the event of any attempt at forced entry into the car. The alarm also responds to any attempt to lift or push the car. Once the alarm is activated, the hazard warning lights and the horn come on for 30 seconds. After this time, a flashing light indicates that the system has been activated.

Engine and gearbox

The fitting of a supercharger to the Cooper S engine resulted in 163bhp at 6,000rpm, a considerable improvement over the 115bhp output of the normally aspirated Cooper. Apart from the big improvement in performance figures – the Mini Cooper manages

0–62mph in 9.6 seconds, the S in 7.4 seconds – it also means that the engine produces over 100bhp per litre, an achievement that the S shares with the E46 BMW M3. The advantage of using a supercharger as opposed to a turbocharger is that there is no turbo lag to delay throttle response. As a result the power delivery in the S is exceptionally smooth and progressive. Torque peaks at 155lb/ft at 4,000rpm, with 80 per cent of the maximum torque being available between 2,000 and 6,500rpm.

When high power outputs are needed from a relatively small engine, forced induction using a supercharger or turbocharger is a very effective method of achieving it. The supercharger fitted to the S is a Roots blower, which is a type normally used in high speed engines requiring relatively low supercharge pressures. It is based on a design patented in America around 1865 by F.M. and P.H. Roots, which was used for a number of purposes including ventilating mines. It is driven by a Poly V-belt. Within the supercharger two rotary pistons or lobes working in opposite directions compress (or, strictly speaking, displace) the incoming air to a maximum overpressure of 0.8 bar. The compression causes the air to heat up, which therefore has to be cooled by the intercooler before entering the combustion chambers. Forced induction produced in this way provides a significant increase in engine power as combustion occurs. The intercooler is supplied with air from the air scoop on the bonnet.

Supercharged power units can be prone to engine knock but this is overcome on the S engine by reducing the compression ratio to 8.3:1 (from 10.6:1). An Active Knock Control system also monitors the combustion process, enabling the engine to run smoothly on unleaded fuel with an octane rating of anything between 91 and 98. This permits the same engine set-up in all markets throughout the world, regardless of the quality of the available fuel.

Though the basic New Mini engine design is the same in the S as in the rest of the range, a number of strengthening modifications have been made to cope with the additional power, and the crankshaft, connecting rods, pistons, engine bearings, and valves have been uprated. An oil cooler, albeit a very small one, is fitted, plus there is splash oil cooling for the pistons. A different uprated exhaust system is also used with twin exhaust tailpipes. The battery has been moved from the engine bay to the rear of the car to counterbalance the supercharger and maintain weight

The S power unit with the front mounted supercharger with intercooler on top. (BMW Press)

The intercooler gives the game away, but just in case people don't know what the engine is there's a small 'S' badge.

distribution.

The Cooper S successfully complies with all UK emissions legislation. Indeed, its engine is one of the few not requiring secondary air injection or exhaust gas re-circulation in order to comply.

Transmission is taken care of with a specially designed 6-speed Getrag manual gearbox, as the Rover-derived box fitted to the One and Cooper was not capable of handling the torque from the S's supercharged engine.

Running gear

The suspension on the S is Sports Suspension Plus, an uprated version of the Sports package which is standard on the Mini Cooper and optional on One models. There are stiffer springs, with reinforced anti-roll bars on both front and rear axles to further improve handling and reduce body roll during hard cornering.

In common with all New Minis, the Cooper S is fitted with disc brakes all round, the front discs being vented. The system is uprated but the discs themselves are the same as those fitted to other models in the range (276

DID YOU KNOW?

If there's not enough room in your Mini Cooper or Cooper S, Corrozzeria Castagna – a firm of coachbuilders based in Milan, Italy – will convert it into an Estate version. A woody effect version is also available for original Mini Traveller fans.

x 22mm at the front and 259 x 10mm at the rear). The electronic safety systems are present too, four-sensor ABS, EBD, and CBC being joined by ASC+T to prevent wheelspin – something that can be achieved without trying in the S. Dynamic Stability Control (DSC) is also available as an option.

The Mini Cooper S is the first car in its class to be fitted with run-flat tyres and a tyre pressure indicator as standard, although a hint of nostalgia creeps in here as the Mini 1275GT from the late 1970s had standard Dunlop Denovo run-flat tyres. Technology has moved on considerably since then and the Cooper S's tyres have reinforced side walls and are made from heat-

Raring to go, the S needs plenty of space to exploit its performance fully.

resistant rubber. Safety functions such as ABS, ASC+T, or DSC are not affected if the tyre pressure drops or is lost altogether and it is possible to continue the journey for up to 80 miles at speeds of up to 50mph. Even if fully deflated, the tyres can safely run at 30mph.

On the road

The first thing that will strike the driver when driving away briskly in a Cooper S will be the sound. The first thing that will strike the passenger will be the grin on the driver's face. The supercharger produces a very distinctive and pleasant sounding whine – drive the S fast and make use of the incredibly slick and fast gearchange, and from inside the sound is not dissimilar to that heard when watching a video taken from inside a rally car round a special stage. The car is by no means noisy – the engine runs very quietly – but the noise it produces creates a lot of 'feel-good factor'.

The S is fitted with ASC+T as standard. Switch it off – at least you can, unlike some cars – and pull away fast and you will soon see why: it's all too easy to smoke the front tyres. The handling is great. The lower, stiffer springs mean that bumps in the road are a lot more noticeable than in the Cooper, but from a handling point of view the price is well worth it. The incredibly stiff body structure comes into its own, further contributing to the pin sharp handling. 0–62mph in 7.4 seconds may not sound especially quick when compared to some high performance cars, but the S feels a lot quicker. This is a true Mini thing; the original Minis always felt quicker than they really were.

Combined fuel consumption of 33.6mpg is impressive for these performance levels. However, this is very much a performance car, and one where you simply feel obliged to use that performance as much of the time as is possible. When you do, the consumption suffers and will easily drop into the low 20s or even less if the car is put through its paces around a track.

The performance of the S – or, to be more exact, the way that the performance is delivered – makes it a somewhat frustrating car to drive in traffic, and owners living in low traffic density areas will be able to enjoy their cars a great deal more.

MINI COOPER S STANDARD EQUIPMENT

Anti-lock Brake System (ABS)
Cornering Brake Control (CBC)
Automatic Stability Control and Traction (ASC+T)
Crash Sensor
Disc brakes all round, ventilated at front
Electronic Braking Distribution (EBD)
Run-flat tyres 195/55R16V
Tyre Defect Indicator
Two front and two side airbags
Three-point safety belts with pre-tensioners and belt force limiters
Chrome door handles
Electric door mirrors in matt black
Third brake light
Tinted glass
50:50 split folding rear seats
Kaleido cloth upholstery
Front and rear cupholders
Digital clock
Easy entry function
Frameless electric front windows
Electro Hydraulic power steering
Height adjustable driver's seat
Height adjustable steering wheel

Thatcham CAT 1 Remote control alarm
Radio cassette with six speakers
Remote central locking
16in Alloy X-lite wheels
Footwell lights
Rev counter
Sports Suspension
Stainless steel mesh grille
White or black roof and wing mirrors
6-speed gearbox
Aluminium look interior trim
Bonnet air intake
Boot handle and radiator grille in body colour
Chrome fuel filler cap
Chrome-plated side repeater grilles
Intercooler
Leather steering wheel and gearknob
Roof spoiler in roof colour
Sport front and rear bumpers
Sports seats
Sports Suspension Plus
Supercharger
Twin chrome exhaust tailpipes
White side indicators

Chapter **Seven**

The Mini Convertible

If the Mini is a fashion statement then a Convertible Mini takes the situation one step further. It just has to be one of the ultimate summer fun cars. In Cooper S form maybe the ultimate. All New Minis feel a lot faster than they actually are due to the low centre of gravity and the directness of the steering; remove the roof and the rush of air over the car will only serve to multiply that feeling. Take a Mini Convertible to the South of France or the Italian lakes in the summer, and with the roof down it will be hard to beat. What's more, park one in the right location and it's going to command as much respect as a Porsche and will certainly attract more attention.

The new Mini Cooper Convertible, looking very cool with the roof down.

The Convertible was introduced in June 2004, making its debut at the 2004 Geneva Motor Show. It is a four-seater in the same way as the steel-roofed models, the rear seats having sensibly not been sacrificed to create the roadster look. The first two models, the Mini One Convertible and Mini Cooper Convertible, became available almost straight away, and the Mini Cooper S Convertible followed in August the same year. The market for compact convertible cars has been very much on the increase in recent times, and in the four years prior to the introduction of the Mini Convertible world-wide sales of convertibles in this market sector had tripled. The UK, USA, and Germany are the largest markets for Mini as a whole, and they are also the three most significant markets for small convertible cars and roadsters, so the Mini Convertible makes a great deal of sense.

All three Convertible models are available in a choice of ten exterior paint colours. These include two exclusive colours (Cool Blue and Hot Orange) for the One and Cooper convertibles, and two exclusive Cooper S colours (Hyper Blue and Dark Silver). The roof covering is black on the Mini One but is available in a choice of three colours – black, blue, or green – on Cooper models. The door mirrors are black on the One in line with the saloon models but are body-coloured on the Cooper.

Newly introduced with the Convertible were redesigned front and rear bumpers. Fitted to the One and Cooper models, these have become standard across the range. Cooper S models, however, retain the original Sports style bumpers. Redesigned headlights also feature on the Convertible and following its introduction also extend across the range. The central locking operates on the doors and boot lid in the usual Mini fashion, but on the Convertible it also operates the fuel flap, the windows, the sliding roof, and the roof as a whole.

The boot lid hinges downwards on Convertible models in the style of the original Mini. The luggage carrying capacity is quoted as 165 litres with the rear seats up and the roof up (which is an increase of 15

The ideal holiday car.

Design sketches of the Mini Convertible. (BMW Press)

Roof up or down, the Convertible top suits the Mini
design well. (BMW Press)

litres over the fixed-roof models), 120 litres with the seats up and the roof down, and 605 litres with the roof up and the rear seats folded. Therefore carrying capacity is not severely compromised by the convertible roof. The BMW Easy Load system connects the luggage compartment with the boot area when the roof is up.

The doors utilise the same frameless windows. Chrome line finishing is available as an option on the Convertible too, the main difference being that on the Convertible the chrome plating is extended to include the rear seat rollbars.

The standard upholstery in all three versions is cloth, with leather options. The dashboard finish is available in silver and anthracite with further options of wood and aluminium. A rev counter is standard across the range.

Bodyshell structure

The Mini Convertible has been designed in such a way that it does not require a B post. BMW also say that the structure is so stiff that it will handle in exactly the same way as the saloon versions. Certainly BMW are very good at making stiff convertible bodyshells, one of the best examples being the E46 3 Series which is completely devoid of scuttle shake.

Safety is very important and is a major selling point in current cars. With a convertible body safety becomes even more important due to the lack of such protection as would normally be provided by the roof. The roof of any car contributes a great deal to the stiffness and structure of the shell, and to compensate for the lack of its steel roof the Mini Convertible has reinforced side sills. This helps to minimise scuttle shake and to prevent deformation of the shell in the event of both frontal and side impacts. An extra strong floorpan, additional crossbars, and thicker body panels have also been designed in at all critical points. The front end of the car is identical in structure to the fixed roof model

The Convertible interior.

and gives equally good results in front-end collision tests.

To protect the occupants in the event of a roll the A pillars are reinforced with a high strength steel tube which has the capability to absorb 1½ times the mass of the car. There is also a roll bar made of high strength aluminium built into and around each of the rear head restraints. This serves as a roadster style styling feature which fits in well with the Mini design, as well as a safety feature.

Additional protection for the occupants is provided by the four standard airbags. There are two airbags at the front plus two built into the front seat side panels. These are important on the saloon models but perhaps even more so on the Convertible. The side head/thorax airbags shield the front seat occupants' head and upper body in the event of a side impact.

The roof

With the roof in the closed position the Mini Convertible sits slightly lower than fixed roof New Minis. Although it does look better with the roof down,

Cutaway convertible bodyshell. Shell rigidity and occupant safety are both excellent. (BMW Press)

as is the case with most convertibles, it still looks good with the roof up, the curves of the lower body complementing the fabric roof. The roof itself is rather unique in that it features an integrated sliding element which can be set to any position within its range before continuing on to form part of the complete folding roof. Both are electrically operated at the touch of a button and the entire roof opens or stows in 15 seconds. The sliding element can be opened at speeds of up to 75mph to its maximum open position of 40mm. There are no catches to be released prior to pressing the operating button, which makes operation of the sliding roof safe when the vehicle is travelling.

The roof folds to the rear, the pillars and the rear side windows retracting automatically into the body of the car, all at the same time. It folds into three layers in a Z formation and stows itself behind the rear seats. The

Even with the roof up the Convertible still looks good.

folding mechanism has been designed to stow it as compactly as possible to minimise the reduction in luggage space, and judging by the figures released by BMW and quoted above it does this very successfully. There is also no need for a tonneau cover as the roof is designed in such a way that its front section creates a cover and protects the roof lining.

The roof also incorporates a glass rear window, which is heated. Rear visibility is reduced slightly due to the rear window and rear side windows being smaller in the fabric roof than in steel-roofed models, but Park Distance Control is fitted as standard equipment throughout the Convertible range to help overcome this.

Engines and gearboxes

Three engine options are available to correspond with the model line up: the 90bhp, the 115bhp, and the 170bhp S engine, as per the rest of the range. There is no diesel option. Although diesel convertibles are beginning to appear on the market it is probably unlikely that a diesel unit will appear in a car as small as a New Mini.

For a long time prior to the launch of the Convertible it had been rumoured that the Chrysler-derived 1.6-litre engine would be replaced with a Peugeot unit, which would then be fitted to the rest of the New Mini range. This did not happen, but there was a major mechanical change to two models in the line-up in that the Rover-derived gearbox was replaced with a five speed Getrag in the One and Cooper Convertibles. The Getrag 'box was fitted to the fixed roof models at the same time and provided slightly improved torque and bhp figures, the power output of the Cooper S being increased to 170bhp at 6,000rpm. This means an additional 7bhp.

The Cooper S Convertible achieves 0–62mph in 7.4

Here's looking at you. S class – open-air Mini motoring at its best.

MINI CONVERTIBLE STANDARD EQUIPMENT

Fully automatic roof with sliding roof function
Four airbags
Four disc brakes
ABS
CBC
EBD
Electrohydraulic power steering
Tyre Defect Indicator
Glass heated rear window
Rear seat headrest folding forward in split configuration, lockable in position
Easy Load function
Lockable glove compartment
Park Distance Control
Remote central locking
Centrally locked fuel filler flap
Electric windows front and rear
Electrically operated exterior mirrors
Colour-coded bumpers

seconds and accelerates from 50–75mph in fourth gear in 6.6 seconds. Top speed is 134mph and fuel consumption is 32.1mpg. Very good with the roof down!

The One Convertible's top speed is 109mph and 0–62 takes 11.8 seconds. The Cooper can achieve 120mph and gets from 0–62 in 9.8 seconds. Fuel consumption for these models is quoted as 39.2 and 38.7mpg respectively in the combined cycle.

Running gear

The Mini One Convertible is fitted with 15in steel wheels in line with the other One models, although being a Convertible it is highly unlikely that many, if indeed any, will be purchased without the alloy wheel option. The Cooper Convertible is fitted with 15in alloy rims of a seven hole design as standard. Both models are fitted with 175/65 R15 tyres. The Cooper S Convertible comes with the 16in X-lite alloy wheels from the fixed roof S as standard. The alloy wheel options from the rest of the range are also available on the Convertible models, plus there is an additional design of 17in alloy wheel, the Bullet, which is exclusive to the Convertible. Both 16in and 17in alloys are fitted with run-flat tyres.

Chapter Eight

The John Cooper Works Coopers

For most New Mini buyers the standard Mini Cooper and Cooper S, as produced by the factory, will be quite fast enough for their requirements. The Cooper is brisk, the S very quick; both are most enjoyable cars in their different ways. As I have already stated, all Minis have an inbuilt tendency to feel faster than they actually are, and this has a lot to do with why they are enjoyable.

The characteristic is a benefit in the standard Mini One and the higher performance Cooper versions alike, but the effect is enhanced and possibly even magnified when the engine is tuned. There are a number of companies – particularly in Britain, Germany, and the

A Mini Cooper S Works.

USA – which offer a variety of tuning packages for all the models in the New Mini range, but there's only one which has official BMW backing to produce faster Coopers which still retain their full manufacturers' warranty. That company is John Cooper Works.

Historically the link between Cooper and Mini goes back to 1961 with factory produced Minis. This link ended in 1971, but was reborn in 1990 when a bolt-on tuning package was developed and sold by what was then John Cooper Garages; when fitted by a Rover dealer, this retained its manufacturers' warranty. The tuning kit was further developed into a Cooper S pack for the reintroduced Mini Cooper, and this S pack was available for fitment to original Minis until production ceased. It is still available for retro fitting even today. This story has already been covered in an earlier chapter, but I mention it again here because it paved the way for today's conversions on the new Coopers.

The Mini has played a big part in making Cooper one of the best-known names in the automotive world and beyond, and this is something of which the team at John Cooper Works – led today by Mike Cooper – is very proud. However, Cooper goes back a lot further than this. Buy a New Mini Cooper or S, especially a Works tuned one, and you become the owner of a modern performance car with a quite exceptional racing and tuning pedigree behind it. Here is just a small taster as to why.

The roots of the story date back to 1934, when Charles Cooper ran a small garage in Surbiton, Surrey, which he started originally to maintain racing cars. His son John Cooper was born in 1923 and his life was destined to revolve around cars and motor racing almost from the day he was born. John's automotive career started when, at only eight years old, he was given a Francis-Barnett engined chain-driven single-seater Special, built by his father. John spent many an hour driving this around in the garage premises, and also at various carnivals and events. The Special had a top speed of about 35–40mph, which was fast in 1923 (it was the top speed of some production cars, and is fast even today for an eight-year-old).

A few years later, when John was 12, the Special was replaced by the car that became known as the 'Number One Cooper Special'. This was also built by his father. It was powered this time by a highly tuned Austin Seven engine, making it considerably faster than the first Special, with a top speed of 90mph. John drove it around the paddock and on the access roads at the various race meetings he attended with his father. He even tried the car out around Brooklands circuit – unofficially, of course.

The Cooper Car Company was formed in the late 1940s, and John Cooper together with Eric Brandon began designing and building the first 'production' Cooper race car. This was powered by a JAP Speedway motorcycle engine, and used a number of running gear components from a Fiat 500 Topolino, mainly because there was a crashed one at the rear of the garage. The whole front end of the Fiat was used, and the leaf spring and wishbone suspension assembly proved so suitable that a similar set-up was used on all production Coopers right up until 1955. The design of the car began with laying out all the components on the floor of the garage.

This first car, the Cooper 500, was tested along the Kingston Bypass in Surrey on the outskirts of London early in the mornings, with a makeshift silencer bolted on to keep the noise to an acceptable level and with trade plates fitted to keep the local constabulary happy. After that the 500 race car was used mainly for hill climbing at Prescott, where it participated in its first official competitive event, and at Shelsley. It was also entered in the Brighton Speed Trials, which was particularly significant since it was at Brighton that John Cooper, in the Cooper 500, beat Alec Issigonis in his racer, the Lightweight Special.

By the end of the second racing season in 1947 a number of enthusiasts had seen the Cooper perform well and had enquired about obtaining a replica. The result was a decision to build a dozen 500cc Coopers. With a top speed of 108mph and a 0–60 time of eight seconds, these cars were quick for their day, and all 12 sold immediately, one of the first customers being Stirling Moss. The racing successes continued, and in the early 1950s the Cooper Car Company built a number of front-engined sports cars, mainly powered by MG engines, and later on by Bristol engines. In all a total of 91 different Cooper models was produced.

In 1959 Formula Junior was introduced. The idea behind it was to build a race car powered by a 1,000cc production engine which had to come from a model of car of which at least 5,000 examples had been made.

DID YOU KNOW?

Although many highly tuned and quick cars have been produced and converted by Cooper over the years, the John Cooper S Works is the first with a supercharged engine.

John decided that the Cooper Car Company would build Formula Junior cars and he visited Donald Healey, who took him to see Alec Issigonis, who handed over a couple of dozen 'A' series 948cc MG Midget engines (tuned versions of the engines used in the Austin A40). The Formula Junior immediately became one of the most successful Cooper race cars, and continued to win races right up until 1964, when the Formula was reborn as Formula 3. Formula Junior is very significant to the Mini story, for it was from the Formula Junior engine that the original Mini Cooper engine was developed. Success continued with F3, and in 1964 the Formula 3 World Champion title was won in a Cooper. The driver's name was Jackie Stewart.

During this time Cooper Cars had moved up in the world and were also having big successes in both Formula 1 and Formula 2. Fitted with Coventry Climax engines specially developed by Wally Hassan, Harry Mundy, and Peter Windsor Smith, under the leadership of Leonard Lee, Cooper cars driven by Jack Brabham took the Formula 1 World Championship in both 1959 and 1960.

The Cooper Car Company did not just build successful racing cars. They were also responsible for starting the first racing drivers' school. This was organised at Brands Hatch, and the first advertisement for the school in *Autosport* magazine attracted a staggering 2,000 replies. Instructors included Jack Brabham and Bruce Maclaren, and also Jim Russell, who liked the idea so much that he later set up his own school.

Mini Coopers and Ss were raced throughout the 1960s, and an early association was formed with the BMC Competitions department at Abingdon whereby financial and material support was provided by BMC which enabled Cooper to represent it in saloon car racing. This left BMC free to concentrate on rallying. Following the Leyland take-over of BMC the Cooper Racing Team was closed down at the end of 1969, along with the Cooper factory premises which were located at Canada Road in Byfleet. It was at this point that John Cooper Garages at Ferring, near Worthing in Sussex, was opened up. During the 1990s the revival of the Mini Cooper increased trade to the extent that a separate Mini Cooper Centre was built at East Preston to deal with the Mini side of the business, a short distance from the main John Cooper Garages' Honda dealership premises.

With a pedigree of racing and specialist performance development extending all the way to Formula 1, it is

unsurprising that BMW chose not only to continue with the Cooper name for the faster models in the New Mini range but also to develop and produce the specialist conversions described in this chapter.

With the arrival of the New Mini came a new company name, John Cooper Works. The word 'Works' was highly relevant, 'the Works team' having been the name given to the Cooper Car Company's own racing drivers back in the 1950s and 1960s and to the Mini teams. Now Cooper Works conversion kits were to become available for both the New Mini Cooper and the Cooper S. There is also, in true tradition, a new racing series for the tuned versions of both models (covered in detail in Chapter 12).

These upgrades for the New Mini were developed by John Cooper Works in conjunction with BMW, the development team being led by JCW's top engine man Tony Franks. The conversion kits are supplied only by John Cooper Works, but they can be fitted either by JCW or by a franchised BMW Mini dealer. Many owners choose to have the kits fitted at JCW in East Preston on the grounds that it makes their car seem just that bit more special. John Cooper Works will sell new Works cars, or alternatively a New Mini dealer supplied car that has already been purchased can be taken down to them for conversion. JCW do not themselves sell new standard Minis or standard Coopers. Their involvement is strictly with the Cooper side of the New Mini, and because of this they do not sell packages for the Mini One.

Mini Cooper Works

The first of the Works Minis, the Mini Cooper Works, was launched in November 2001, just four months after the Mini Cooper itself was launched by BMW. The conversion kit had been developed at the same time as the New Mini, and had taken the development team at Cooper nearly three years to perfect – in the late 1990s BMW had enlisted the help of John and Mike Cooper and their team to develop not only the production cars but also the higher performance conversions too.

The Cooper Works conversion retains the full BMW Mini warranty. This is particularly reassuring to owners, and is certainly a very good reason to go for this conversion rather than an aftermarket kit if buying a new or a nearly new Mini which still has plenty of warranty left. Additional peace of mind comes from the fact that the conversions were comprehensively tested before they were launched, in much the same way that new cars are put through their paces. This involved operating them in extremes of temperature plus covering many miles under differing conditions to ensure reliability. In the case of the Works Minis this added up to 150,000 miles of durability testing and 20,000 miles of high speed testing. This was carried out all over the world and at racing circuits such as Spa, Goodwood, and the BMW Williams test track. This type of testing is necessary if a warranty is to remain in place, since reliability and longevity are as important as the increase in performance.

The Cooper Works – officially called at launch the John Cooper Works Mini Cooper – falls between the

Cooper and Cooper S. At the time of its launch the Cooper S was not yet available, and the Works Cooper was consequently the fastest BMW-backed Mini available, as well as being the fastest New Mini available at the time. The Works conversion package consists of a mixture of traditional tuning components and electronic tuning. There is nothing radical involved. It simply fine tunes the engine to extract smooth, usable, extra power. In old-fashioned tuning language it would probably fit in somewhere between a Stage One and Two kit. There are no tractability penalties and no call for 4,000 revs just to pull away.

At the heart of the conversion is a modified cylinder head. This is a new casting and new components, not an exchange item. The head is modified traditionally by grinding away metal to reshape the inlet and exhaust ports in order to improve the flow characteristics. JCW say that the inlet ports have been reshaped to allow the gases to flow into the cylinders in as straight a line as possible. As with any cylinder head modification, the amount of metal removed is critical – remove too little and there is minimal advantage, remove too much and power will be lost. In the case of the Cooper head more work has to go into the exhaust side than the inlet, and in total around 20 hours is spent on each head. This

The Cooper Works engine.

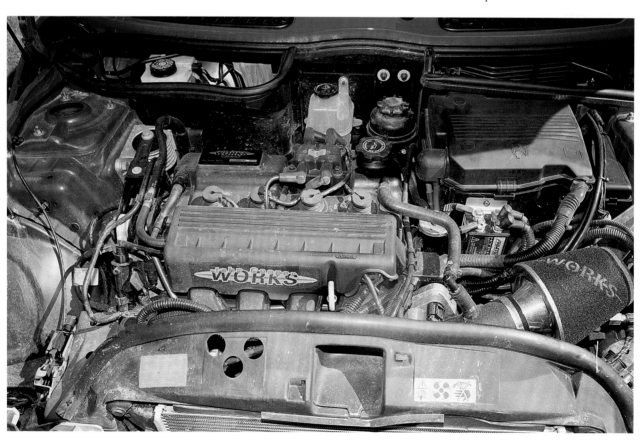

includes matching the ports to the manifolds. The heads are CNC machined and computer-aided design was used extensively in their development.

As well as the improvements to gas flow the compression ratio is raised slightly, from the 10.6:1 of the standard Cooper to 10.9:1. The cylinder head mods make up in the region of a 12bhp increase in power. The rest of the power is obtained by fitting a less restrictive air filter assembly and a freer flowing stainless steel exhaust system from the catalytic converter backwards. The tailpipe is fitted with a chrome-plated finisher and looks considerably more aggressive than the standard fitment. The system not only helps to improve power, but also changes the note of the engine, making it sound very much more purposeful. The standard exhaust manifold remains as it is – to change it would involve the catalytic converter and would affect emissions.

The engine is also remapped, and a CD is supplied with the conversion for this purpose. The remapping is necessary so as to bring the management side of the engine in line with the modifications that have been made, but there are also changes to the way that the engine responds. These give improved throttle response and more mid-range torque. The car is still very smooth, but is much more willing to rev. There is also more power higher up the range. On paper the performance increase doesn't sound particularly massive, but it does make a real difference to the acceleration and driveability of the car. Because it is BMW backed the Cooper Works has been tested by BMW and the official 0–62mph time is 8.9 seconds.

There are no suspension modifications. Being a Cooper the Mini Sports Suspension is fitted, making the car lower and stiffer anyway. The suspension handles the extra power easily and shows off the capabilities of the standard system, and although there is no reason why an owner should not improve the handling further by carrying out mods there is no actual need to do so. As stated earlier, the Mini Cooper excels through fast corners anyway: the extra power just makes it that extra bit more fun.

As a finishing touch to the package subtle but nonetheless important John Cooper Works badges are added on the two dummy grilles on each front wing and also on the bootlid. There are also two Works badges, one included on the identifying plate located under the bonnet. Many Cooper Works cars are supplied with a BMW bodykit and numerous other additional accessories. A large range is a available from Cooper.

The Mini Cooper Works Conversion takes one full day to fit. At the time of writing it is readily available through John Cooper Works, is listed and detailed in the BMW Mini Accessories Brochure, and is fitted to the John Cooper Challenge race series cars. Well over 100 conversions have been carried out, but fitting of the Cooper Works package to road-going cars has slowed down somewhat since June 2002 for a very good reason. This was when the 163bhp Cooper S was launched. The price difference between the S and the Cooper Works was minimal, and the standard S was far quicker. But then the S Works was introduced, and that was quicker still …

Driving impressions: Cooper Works

The Mini Cooper is, in standard form, a relatively mild-mannered car. This is not to say that it is slow or boring in any way; it is not. But it could never generate the level of excitement provided by the fast acceleration of the S, since it was never designed to do this in the first place. Some owners may wish that their Mini Cooper was just that bit faster, but do not want the full-on hot hatch performance of the S. The answer for such

The Works air filter system upgrade.

The Works engine is identified by a numbered plaque.

The S Works conversion is equally at home on road or track.
(BMW Press)

owners is, without a doubt, the Mini Cooper Works conversion. Adding the Cooper Works package to the Mini Cooper makes quite a difference, and that difference is a lot more noticeable when the car is driven than it is on paper.

Looking at the performance figures it would be easy to think that it wouldn't be easy to spot the difference between a standard Cooper and a Works, but this is not the case at all. Right from the beginning, when the engine is fired up, there is the exhaust note. It is quite a bit racier and just a bit noisier thanks to the modified freer flowing system, and this immediately makes the car feel more powerful. But there is a great deal more to the Works than that.

The Mini One and the Cooper have both come in for some mild criticism in the engine department, on the grounds that the latter tends to become slightly coarse when it is pushed hard. The improved torque band of the Works Cooper helps to overcome this. There is still plenty of the low-down torque that is a feature of the standard car but the Works Cooper has more torque higher up the rev range. This is probably due as much

as anything to the gas flow improvements to the cylinder head. The uprated engine is generally much more willing to rev and throttle response is improved, making for a racier engine altogether. The revs fall away faster too.

The handling of the Cooper is good in standard form, and remains good with the extra power of the Works Conversion. The modifications made to the Mini One suspension to create the Sports Suspension package, fitted as standard to the Cooper by the factory, are ideal for this conversion. To sum up, the Cooper Works package makes a good car more drivable and a lot more fun – a great conversion for the cherished weekend car and high mileage everyday car alike.

Mini Cooper Works v standard Cooper performance figures

Model	0–62mph	50–75mph	Top speed (4th gear)
Cooper	9.2 secs	10.5 secs	125mph
JCW Cooper	8.9 secs	10.1 secs	126mph

Mini Cooper S Works

For the vast majority of Mini Cooper S buyers their car will be quite fast enough in standard form. It is the ultimate fun car in its class and has been hailed as such on many occasions by the motoring press. But there are some owners who seek even more power and enjoyment from their cars, which is why the Cooper S Works was created.

If the standard S is the ultimate in its class then the S Works must surely represent the ultimate even when competing against cars several classes up. Available from April 2003 and coming with a full BMW warranty, the S Works conversion package turns a fast Mini into a seriously fast Mini. It was developed in much the same way as the Cooper package and took a similar length of time to perfect. Once again extensive testing was carried out before the product was launched, including extreme temperatures ranging from 35°C right down to minus 20°C, which should cover the temperature bands likely to be encountered by the majority of people wanting to drive a performance Mini!

The Cooper S Works is modelled along the same lines as the Cooper version. There are no drastic modifications to the engine, no massive overbores or uprated camshafts, and all of the uprated parts are bolt-on. This means that the S package can be fitted by JCW or by any franchised Mini dealer, although some Mini dealers prefer to send their cars down to JCW for the work to be carried out.

Like the Cooper Works, at the heart of the Cooper S Works is the modified cylinder head. This is modified along broadly similar lines to the Cooper Works head: work is done to the inlet and exhaust ports and the chambers are slightly reworked and polished. Comparing it with a standard head the difference is immediately noticeable, although, once again, too much metal cannot be removed or the performance gain is reversed. The modified head is a brand new component rather than being supplied on an exchange

The interior of the Works cars is unaltered.

Above: The S Works is a dramatic car.

Right: The Cooper S Works, capable of burning up most other cars.

Below: The rear end of the S Works, the view that most people will see.

basis – the Works conversion is carried out on brand new or virtually new cars, so fitting used components – even if they have only covered 100 miles – is not an option. Valve sizes in the modded head are the same as the standard car, and the camshaft is also the standard item.

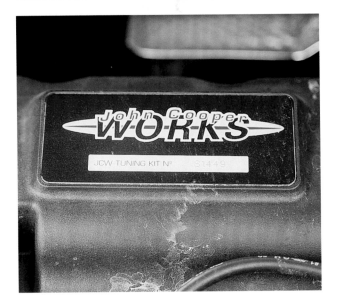

Above: The **S** Works engine with revised intercooler cover.

Left: There is an **S** Works badge on the intercooler too.

Below: The **S** Works numbered identification plate.

What makes the big difference to the S, though, is the modified supercharger. The main modification is a different driving wheel, but internal mods are also carried out as the supercharger spins faster on the Works S. The result is that supercharger boost is up from .7 bar to 1.0 bar. A new drive belt is also supplied in the conversion. The exhaust system is replaced from the cat back, and again the standard exhaust manifold is retained for emissions reasons. The replacement exhaust is noticeably faster looking than the standard item – although it actually has an additional silencer it is very much a straight-through. It uses a parallel flow low back pressure system, tuned not only for improved engine performance but for improved aural pleasure both inside and outside the car. It doesn't make the car sound noisy, just nice, and the S Works passes all noise and emissions regulations easily.

The engine is remapped to adjust the management system to the modified components and to get the best out of the changed specification. Perhaps the most amazing thing about the Mini Cooper S is that even with this conversion, which adds 37bhp to the power output, the only parts changed are engine components. There are no changes to the suspension or brakes. Everything, including springs, dampers, discs, and pads, remains completely standard.

The Mini Cooper S Works is identified externally by a badge on the mesh grille by the front number plate, by badges on the imitation grilles at the sides, and by the badge on the bootlid on the opposite side to the Cooper S badge. In the engine compartment there is a larger intercooler cover which is again badged, and an identification plate is fixed behind this to the left of the cooling system reservoir. At the rear the twin chromed Works inscribed exhaust pipes give the game away too.

Mini Cooper S Works v standard S performance figures

Model	0–62mph	50–75mph	Top speed (4th gear)
Cooper S	7.4 secs	6.7 secs	135mph
JCW Cooper S	6.7 secs	5.6 secs	140mph

Top: External badging is very subtle. This is the lower grille badge at the front.

Middle: The rear badge is subtle too.

Bottom: This badge lets you know what you're getting yourself into.

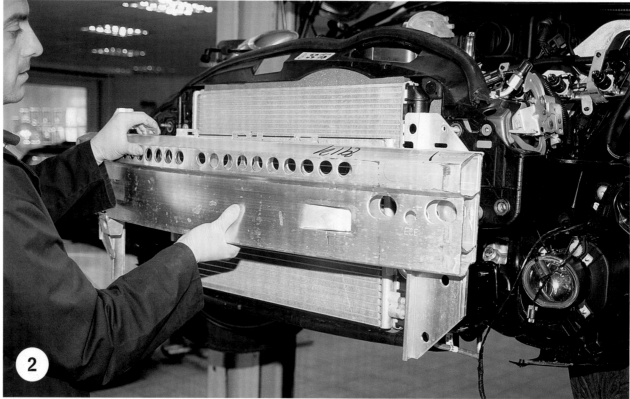

Picture story: how a Cooper S Works is converted

The work required to turn a standard Cooper S into a John Cooper Works S takes one-and-a-half days. There are many steps involved in the process, and the following sequence only covers the main ones. To cover the entire process in detail would take a whole chapter. The changing of the main components to the upgraded items is carried out in the following manner:

1: A new Cooper S has been driven into the John Cooper Works workshop. First of all the front end is removed to allow easy access to the engine components. The entire front bumper and lower grille assembly can be removed in well under half an hour.

2: The next task is to remove the aluminium crossmember bolted on in front of the radiator, and the air conditioning condenser where fitted.

3: The air con condenser can be carefully moved to one side and supported to avoid disturbing the system – the condenser is linked to the rest of the system by flexible hoses to enable this. The cooling system is drained and the radiator removed.

4: With these components removed and with the bonnet up the car looks very stripped out.

5: After removing various components, such as the intercooler and drive belts, the inlet manifold is removed from the cylinder head. This allows access to the supercharger.

6: The supercharger assembly is removed, complete with the air intake.

7: The difference in the supercharger pulleys can clearly be seen in this picture of original and uprated superchargers. The supercharger with the smaller pulley is the uprated Works item.

8: The timing chain is released from the pulley at one end of the cylinder head and the head is then removed from the engine. The block face is cleaned up – only very minimal cleaning is required on a new engine. A new head gasket is fitted.

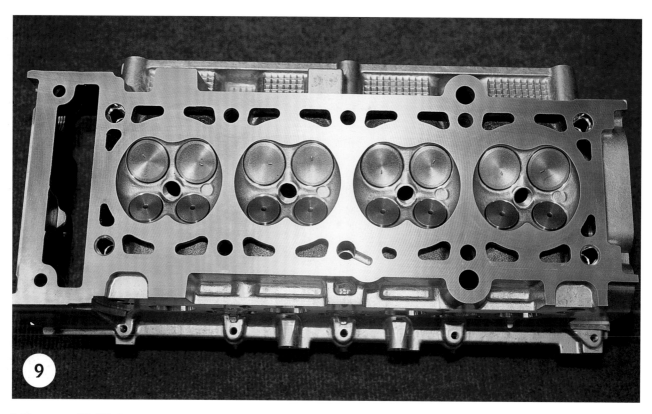

9: The new modified Works cylinder head. The chambers are lightly modified and polished, which looks good, but most of the grinding and reshaping work is carried out on the inlet and exhaust ports and is therefore internal.

10: The head is fitted to the car, and the timing wheel and chain refitted in the correct position. This is followed by the new supercharger, which is fitted with the standard air intake from the original supercharger.

11: The intercooler and the JCW casing are fitted. The S works identifying plaque is fitted to the engine. A final check is made for tightness on all nuts and bolts. The radiator is refitted, the air con condenser and front aluminium crossmember also, followed by the front bumper. The radiator is refilled with coolant and the underbonnet side of the conversion is completed.

12: The standard Cooper S exhaust system is removed at the joint with the catalytic converter.

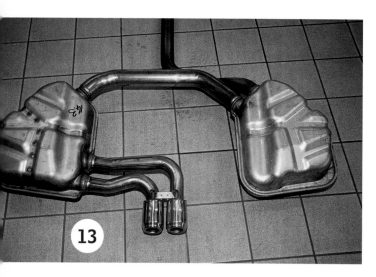

13: This is the standard Cooper S system following removal. On the ground it does look surprisingly restrictive for such a high performance car.

14: The new Works item does look a lot freer flowing. The new system includes an additional silencer which is closer to the engine end and is not shown in this picture.

15: The Works system is fitted and the twin Cooper S Works chromed tailpipes are put on. After this the badges are applied to the bodywork and S Works identifier strips are fitted on to the door steps to alert all passengers that they are entering an S Works Cooper as they climb on board.

16: The conversion is not all mechanical. New software is downloaded into the Mini's management system using a laptop. Rolling road tuning is not necessary, the car being correctly programmed by the downloaded software.

17: Parked outside the John Cooper Works headquarters in East Preston and ready for the road. The completed Cooper S Works is test driven before being collected by its owner.

17

Driving impressions: Cooper S Works

The S Works is an impressive machine. Driving in a small car like a New Mini is always going to be entertaining: the fact that it is a Mini, with the chuckabilty and impressive level of driver involvement coupled with superb handling – those things that basically make a Mini a Mini – only serves to complete the experience. Fire the car up and the S Works upgrade is immediately apparent, the deeper, throatier exhaust note revealing that this is a breathed-on Mini. This exhaust note stays with you all the way through the range and makes the car feel faster than it actually is, even more so than with standard Minis. Upon pulling away there is a very slight hesitation, a small hiccup at low revs fairly early on. This was present in the test car used in preparing this book and was a characteristic of early S Works conversions. JCW say that the engine remapping has since been slightly revised and that this has eliminated the problem on later conversions so that the S Works is now smooth throughout the range. Even with the hiccup (which is not a problem once you become accustomed to it) the car was very smooth, especially for a 1,600cc engine producing this kind of power.

Below: Parked up after an exhilarating drive.

Right: Country roads – indeed any roads – are fun in an S Works.

However, the S Works really comes into its own on winding roads. The power and response from the tuned engine is not so noticeable lower down the range; but it is on song in the mid range. Somehow too the S's suspension seems to work even better with the additional power going through. Very fast acceleration on an undulating country road can produce a slightly light feeling in the steering, though, but this feeling is present on a hard-driven standard car under similar conditions.

The Cooper S Works needs traction control especially in slippery conditions – try pulling away fast with the Traction switched off and it is virtually impossible to avoid wheelspin, and this happens when the power is applied after fast gearchanges in second, third, and fourth too. This is a car for the enthusiast, the competent experienced driver who is capable of handling a performance car. It is not a car for the inexperienced.

Like the standard S it can be frustrating in traffic. It just cries out to be unleashed on the open road where both car and driver can enjoy themselves to the full. You will need to drive a Ferrari or something similar costing many times the price to have anything like as much fun as you can with a Cooper S Works. Having said that it is a car that needs to be driven carefully. The speedometer needs constant monitoring or it could rapidly bring about the loss of your driving licence.

Chapter Nine

New Mini options and accessories

The New Mini has proved to be a very popular and desirable car that continues to sell exceptionally well, and yet despite this popularity it manages to remain very individual. What is more it can be made even more individual – more or less as individual as you want it to be. The standard levels of equipment are very reasonable on every model, but a huge range of options is also available that allows new purchasers to personalise their car according to taste and budget. There are also many genuine New Mini accessories that can be added to both new and used cars, and some of the factory options can also be retro fitted to older cars.

The idea of individualising a new car is not new. It has been common practice in the USA for a long time and probably came to the UK for the first time in the late 1960s, when the Ford Capri was introduced. BMW have nearly always been very strong on options, the basic list price of most of their models being a long way from the average price paid for the cars. However, a large options range was never a feature of the old Mini until 1996, when the car was re-engineered by BMW and was marketed primarily as a fashion accessory rather than an everyday means of transport. The New Mini qualifies as both, and as a result the options help to tailor the car to individual needs and requirements.

The bespoke nature of New Mini production allows mixing and matching of components and equipment, meaning that it is possible to produce tens of

thousands of different Minis, with the cars coming down the production line at any one time all being built to individual specifications. To illustrate this, taking one model – a new Cooper S – as an example, in theory it is possible that every customer for the next four years could have an exclusive car. This makes the Mini unique in its class. Finding a standard New Mini, or indeed any two that are exactly the same, is likely to prove very difficult if it is possible at all – even cars that are built to the same specification are likely to be finished in different colours!

Virtually all of the New Mini options are available individually. There are also combination packs available, which offer a group of popular options at a heavily discounted price and are well worth considering on a new purchase. These are the Salt, Pepper, and Chili packs (described below).

The option and accessories list ranges from roof decals and bonnet stripes to satellite navigation and two different types of air conditioning. The fitting of options really does make a considerable difference and can dramatically alter the character of the car. This became very apparent during the writing of this book, some of the press cars seen being close to standard while others came absolutely laden with extras. The silver Mini Cooper featured in Chapter 5 cost a lot more than the blue Cooper S featured in Chapter 6.

Perhaps one of the best things about the New Mini as far as options go is that virtually all of the options are available across the range. This means that sporty details such as sports seats and Sports Suspension can be

Above right: Body-coloured sills look good on the Cooper S.

Right: Factory options can radically alter the appearance of the new Mini. (BMW Press)

DID YOU KNOW?

BMW say that the list of optional extras and accessories is so large, and the possible number of combinations so great, that there is only a one in 100,000 chance of owning exactly the same Mini as someone else.

specified on a Mini One if the owner so desires. This is particularly good for younger drivers who may not be able to insure or afford one of the higher performance models. It also means that it is possible to have a very sporty and economical car by choosing the Mini One D with a few extras. The hardest things to do are decide exactly what to add and to remain within your budget – most people tend to succumb to temptation! There are certainly plenty of options to consider when buying a New Mini, and plenty more to think about adding afterwards.

There are certain options that make a lot of sense when buying a New Mini. They will enhance the value later on when the car is eventually sold, and make a big difference to enjoyment of the car while you own it. Options of this nature that immediately spring to mind are alloy wheels on the Mini One models, and air conditioning and a leather rim steering wheel on those models not so equipped.

New Mini options

As mentioned above, three different options packages are offered on the New Mini, known as Salt, Pepper, and Chili. The availability of these packages and, to a certain degree, their content depends upon the model involved, not all of the packages being available on every model. These packages involve buying a combination of the most popular options at substantial savings over the cost of buying the extras individually. As an example, the cost saving on the Salt Pack for the Mini One D is around 46 per cent.

The Salt Pack

The Salt Pack is available on the Mini One and Mini One D only. It includes front fog lights, a height adjustable passenger seat, the interior light package, Brilliant Silver interior trim, on-board computer, a rev counter (this is standard on the One D and is reflected in the price of the pack), storage compartment package, and velour floor mats.

The Pepper Pack

The Pepper Pack is available on the Mini One, Mini One D, and Mini Cooper. It includes all of the items included

in the Salt Pack plus 15in eight-spoke alloy wheels and Chrome Line Exterior. Inside there is also a perforated leather steering wheel and gear knob. Again there is a big saving on the cost of the individual options. However, the actual price of this package varies more according to the model to which it is fitted, the main cost difference between models being that alloy wheels are fitted as standard to the Cooper (although they are of a different design, seven-hole being standard on this model).

The Chili Pack

The Chili Pack is available on the Mini Cooper and Mini Cooper S, and includes all the items listed for the Pepper Pack. In addition, on the Mini Cooper the pack includes 16in five-star alloy wheels, cloth/leather Kaleido upholstery, a three-spoke sports leather steering wheel and gear knob, a rear roof spoiler in body colour, sports front seats, and Sports Suspension Plus.

The Chili Pack is upgraded when it is specified on the Mini Cooper S. In addition to the aforementioned items for the Mini Cooper, 17in S-spoke light-alloy wheels replace the standard alloys and cloth/leather Satellite seat coverings replace the Cooper's Kaleido. There is also manual air conditioning and Xenon headlights with headlight washers. The cost saving percentage remains broadly similar to that of the Salt Pack on the Mini One.

Colour choice

Each model of New Mini is available in ten different colours ranging from very traditional to very bright and including a number of metallic finishes. The actual choice varies according to model, most models having two colours that are exclusive to them. The most popular paint choices for all models are Pure Silver, Chili Red, and British Racing Green. Metallic colours are a chargeable option.

Sunroof

For those not requiring a roof decal there is the option of an electrically operated panoramic slide-and-tilt sunroof. This is very large, and opens up to almost one-and-a-half times the size of a conventional sunroof. It also has a back section of solid glass fixed in position behind the opening section, which creates a very spacious atmosphere inside the car.

Rear roof spoiler

A rear roof spoiler is available for the Mini One, One D, Cooper, and Cooper S. It is a very neat fitment which is positioned just above the rear window and effectively forms a small extension to the roof. Needless to say, this spoiler will not fit on Mini Convertible models.

Bonnet stripes

Bonnet stripes reminiscent of the 1960s Cooper Car Co racing Minis and the 1990s Special edition original Mini Coopers are available, and have proved to be very popular on the New Mini. They are available in white, black, silver, or chequered designs.

Automatic transmission

The Mini One and Mini Cooper are both available with automatic transmission in the form of Continuously Variable Transmission (CVT) with Steptronic. CVT provides normal automatic transmission for driving in traffic, and a Sports mode with a six-gear semi-automatic Steptronic transmission. It differs from conventional automatic transmission systems in that it is stepless. Conventional systems use a torque converter, while CVT uses an oil bath multi-disc coupling that is electronically controlled. The transmission itself uses a fixed length steel drive belt to connect two double cone shaped belt pulleys, which transmit the drive from the engine. This provides infinitely variable transmission ratios.

The electronic control comes from the Powertrain Controller, which continuously monitors, and adjusts when necessary, the position of the cone shaped pulleys and ensures that the transmission ratio is exactly right for the driving conditions. The adjustment in position is both smooth and constant, hence the absence of steps. Sports mode is engaged by moving the gear lever from D to S, and is simply a racier version of the continuously variable operation. The transmission automatically changes from Sports mode to Steptronic mode when the driver 'changes gear' manually, which is done by moving the gear lever forwards or back to change up or down in ratio. The shift status is displayed on an LED display located within the speedometer.

In Steptronic mode the main difference from D or S mode is that six electronically fixed ratios are selected, the transmission being limited electronically to six predetermined ratios. The engine can rev higher in this mode, up to 6,000rpm. There is a fail-safe switching system to prevent errors which could cause damage to the engine or the transmission.

Progress from standstill is very smooth with CVT transmission. The electronically controlled coupling does not transmit full power until an engine speed of 2,000rpm has been reached. Power produced is restricted and transmitted evenly.

Steptronic paddles for the steering wheel can be specified at additional cost with automatic transmission.

Suspension upgrades

Sports Suspension

Sports Suspension is fitted as standard to the Mini Cooper. The same suspension package is available as an option which can be specified on the Mini One and One D. It makes a significant difference to the way that the car handles at the expense of a slightly stiffer ride. Sports Suspension consists of 8mm lower springs. The anti-roll bar at the front end is stiffened and an anti-roll bar is also fitted at the rear. The lower ride height improves the car's appearance and makes it look a lot more sporty; many owners specify Sports Suspension for this reason alone.

Sports Suspension Plus

Sports Suspension Plus is simply a further uprated version of the Sports Suspension package which is standard on the Mini Cooper and optional on One models. There are stiffer springs with reinforced anti-roll bars on both front and rear axles to further improve handling and reduce body roll during hard cornering. Sports Suspension Plus is only available as an option on Mini Cooper models. Both Sports Suspension and Sports Suspension Plus are inexpensive options.

Space saver spare wheel

A space saver spare wheel can be specified instead of the Mini Mobility System. Minis with the Mobility system do not carry a spare but instead carry a sealant and a compressor stored in the boot. The sealant is put into the tyre through the valve and pressure can then be restored using the compressor. Some owners prefer to be more traditional and carry a spare, although this option is only available with 15in wheels on Mini One models and the Mini Cooper.

Exterior options

Black bumper inserts

The front and rear bumper inserts on the One and Cooper models are supplied as standard in body colour, but black inserts can be specified at extra cost. However, this option is not available on the Cooper S. Most people opt for the Chrome Line Exterior.

Chrome Line Exterior

Chrome Line Exterior means basically that the bumper inserts are chrome plated. This is a very popular and slightly more retro option and a great many New Minis are to be seen featuring such chrome bumpers. This option is also available on Cooper S models.

Chromed door mirror caps

If you like chrome then why not continue the theme on the door mirrors? This option is available on all models and is inexpensive. Some may feel that the mirrors are too large for this type of treatment, so it is not a bad idea to take a look at a car equipped thus before ordering your own!

The Chrome Line Exterior rear bumper.

Tinted windows

Tinted windows are standard across the whole New Mini range, as they are on virtually every other car made today. Owners who so desire can opt to go a shade further and have a top tinted windscreen. As another separate option, darker tinted glass can also be specified on the other windows.

Interior options

Interior trim

The standard trim to the dashboard areas is Anthracite on the Mini One, One D, and Cooper, and Alloy Patina (aluminium look) on the Cooper S. However, a number of alternatives are available. Alloy Patina can be specified as an extra cost option on One models and on the Cooper, as can Brilliant Silver and Wood Effect, the latter also being available on the Cooper S. Wood Effect trim is by far the most expensive of the finishes. Anthracite and Brilliant Silver are also available as a no extra cost alternative on the Cooper S.

Storage compartment package

This is a low cost option which will help to keep the car tidy. It consists of a glovebox with lid and pockets fitted

There are several dashboard colour options. This is Alloy Patina.

The interior storage compartment package consists of a glovebox and seat pockets.

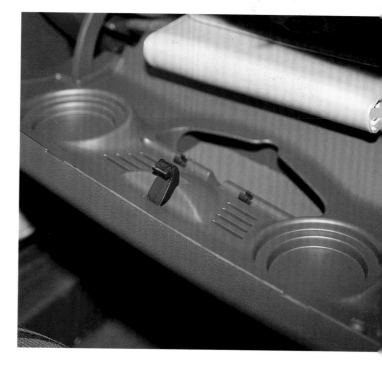

One of the leather upholstery options.

to the rear of the front seats, the pockets being useful for holding road maps or a small atlas.

Leather steering wheel

A two-spoke leather steering wheel, accompanied by a leather gear knob, can be specified on all models

Another leather option, this time shown on the front seats.

except the Cooper S, the latter being fitted with a sports leather steering wheel and gear knob as standard. The sports type leather wheel can also be ordered on the rest of the range. A leather steering wheel and gear knob is included in the Pepper Pack, and also comes as part of the cloth/leather and full leather upholstery options. If your New Mini isn't going to be equipped with a leather steering wheel as a result of having an accessory pack fitted, make sure you specify one as an option. It really does improve the driving pleasure and is absolutely streets ahead of the standard plastic rimmed wheel. An essential extra.

A Multifunction leather steering wheel is also available. This provides direct operation of the stereo system and the cruise control.

Upholstery in cloth/leather or full leather

Cloth/leather combination upholstery is available as an option on all models. It includes the aforementioned leather steering wheel and gear knob, plus lumbar support on the One, One D, and Cooper, where they are not already standard equipment. Full leather upholstery is also available on all models, with the previously mentioned extras where not standard. A leather upgrade can also be specified on the Cooper S in conjunction with the Chili Pack at a reduced price. A large number of Cooper Ss are fitted with the optional leather upholstery, the choices of which include two Satellite cloth/leather combinations and two Gravity full leather upholstery designs. Both are available in lapis blue/black panther or black panther/black panther, while black or blue carpets match the upholstery, creating a very luxurious and upmarket interior.

Sports seats

Sports seats trimmed in cloth are standard on the Mini Cooper S. Similar seats can be fitted to all other models down the range. Sports seats are also available in the cloth/leather combination and full leather.

Heated seats

Two-stage seat heating is available as an option on both driver and front passenger seats. Particularly useful with leather seats in cold climates!

Height adjustment for front passenger seat

The driver's seat is height adjustable on all models. For a relatively small fee this can be extended to the front passenger seat too. Passenger seat height adjustment is included in all three of the accessory packages, Salt,

Pepper, and Chili, so a lot of New Minis will have this included anyway. In considering this option, particularly on the lower priced models, it is worth looking at the whole Salt Pack anyway. The difference in price is not that great.

Safety options

AHPS

The Advanced Head Protection System (AHPS) is an optional head airbag system that extends back from the A to the C pillar. When specified, it is housed within the roof lining along the side. In the event of a collision the airbag will inflate from the A pillar back to the C pillar. All of the New Mini's airbags are controlled by a network of crash sensors.

ASC+T

ASC+T traction control prevents front wheel spin. It uses the ABS sensors to detect any wheel slippage and automatically cuts power to the spinning wheel until it grips again. It can be deactivated by a driver who is looking to take the car to its limits. ASC+T is standard on the Mini Cooper S and the One D and an option on the One and the Cooper.

DSC

Dynamic Stability Control (DSC) is a more sophisticated control system that prevents the car from oversteering or understeering. It increases the safety level to an even higher standard by applying the individual brakes as required if the vehicle becomes unstable whilst accelerating or when pushing through a sharp bend. It is achieved through automatic brake applications to individual wheels and the momentary cutting of power to the engine. The DSC option includes ASC+T.

DSC monitors the ABS speed sensors on the wheels, brake pressure (whether, and how firm, the driver is applying the brakes), the steering wheel lock (to determine the direction the car is travelling), and lateral acceleration acting on the car. It therefore considers both the driver's intentions and the current motion of the car, sensing whether the vehicle is deviating critically from the expected direction of travel. Individual brake applications and changes in the engine torque then correct any deviation.

DSC counteracts oversteer by applying the brake, or increasing the brake pressure if the driver is already braking on the outer front wheel. This reduces pressure on the wheels facing the inside of the bend, allowing them to grip and pull the car through the bend. To counteract understeer, the DSC control unit applies the brake on the inner rear wheel, taking brake pressure off the outer wheels and pulling the car back into the bend. When DSC was specified on pre-July 2004 Mini Ones a rev counter had to be ordered at the same time.

ISOFIX

ISOFIX can be specified for the rear sets. This is very worthwhile for anyone with very young children or anyone considering having children. Correct fitting of child seats is an important safety issue and ISOFIX is one way of ensuring it is done correctly. A range of accessory child seats is available from Mini for both ISOFIX-fitted cars and those not so equipped.

Rear park distance control

Rear visibility is actually quite good on the New Mini, as the rear does not protrude very far beyond the rear window as it does on, for instance, a BMW 3 Series. For those who regularly have to park in tight spaces, or have a small garage, or are just useless at parking, Park Distance Control (PDC) is worthwhile.

Visibility package

The visibility package is a good one for both UK buyers and customers in colder climates. It includes a rain sensor which controls the wipers according to the amount of rain falling onto the windscreen, a heated front windscreen, and an automatic anti-dazzle dimming rear view mirror. Also available separately from this package as another option package are heated washer jets and wing mirrors.

Air conditioning

Air conditioning is one thing that all buyers should seriously consider unless the car is intended for competition purposes or is only being used in a permanently cold climate. It will not only make a significant difference to the resale value of the car but will affect how easy it is to sell in the first place. New Minis hold their value well, but those with air con do it better. Two types of air con are available: manual air conditioning and automatic, which is basically climate control. The latter is around 30 per cent more expensive and, needless to say, is a more versatile and superior system. However, both systems work well.

Alarm system

An optional Thatcham category one alarm system is available. This is a highly desirable extra which will

The factory-fit satellite navigation package.

hopefully help you keep your New Mini and will also help to reduce its insurance premium. The alarm system has its own power supply and is set off immediately upon forced entry into the car. It also responds to any attempt at lifting or pushing the car. Once the alarm is activated, the hazard warning lights

Retro-fit sat nav. (BMW Press)

and the horn are activated for 30 seconds. After this time a flashing light will indicate that the system has been activated.

Satellite navigation

An excellent satellite navigation system is available for the New Mini range. When this is specified, the speedometer is moved from its central position in the dashboard to a new location next to the rev counter in front of the driver. The satellite navigation display then takes the place of the speedo in the central dial. The sat nav in the Mini Cooper press car worked well and proved to be very accurate. However, sat nav systems in general are not absolutely infallible and some roads are not included. It is nevertheless an invaluable tool for anyone needing to find addresses on a regular basis or to navigate through traffic congestion – it is certainly much easier and safer than trying to read a map. It is an expensive option, though, and an update CD must be purchased annually to keep the system up to date. These update CDs, however, are not very expensive. The sat nav system also includes a trip computer and Radio BOOST (see the ICE section below).

Lighting options

There are a number of external lighting options and features. These include halogen front fog lights, a headlamp power wash system, and xenon headlights that also feature an auto-levelling function and lighting distance control. There is also an interior lights

package which consists of footwell lights, map reading lights, and illuminated vanity mirrors.

On-board computer

The New Mini on-board computer provides information on average speed, fuel consumption, outside temperature, and the distance that the car is able to travel with the amount of fuel left on board. The display is located in the rev counter; Mini One models therefore require a rev counter to be specified when this option is selected.

ICE

All New Minis come equipped with a radio cassette player as standard. Six speakers also come as standard, with four mounted in the doors and two in the rear side panels. There is certainly no shortage of upgrade options as far as in-car entertainment is concerned. These include Radio BOOST (which is basically an upgrade of the radio cassette system), a single slot CD radio, a single slot Mini Disc radio, and a six-CD changer fitted in the boot. The ultimate upgrade is a Harman Kardon hi-fi system. All of the CD systems and the Harman Kardon require Radio BOOST to be fitted before they can be specified.

Alloy wheels

A number of different alloy wheel options are available across the New Mini range, with a further exclusive design being available for Convertible models. As the

With the sat nav package, the speedometer moves next to the rev counter in front of the driver.

hubs and brakes are the same throughout the range this means that any wheel can be fitted on any model. The wheels described below are the factory options, but several other designs are available from Mini dealers (these are listed below under accessories).

The rev counter, optional on the Mini One until July 2004.

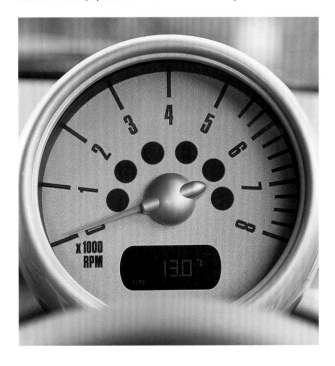

The R85 S-spoke alloy wheel.

15in alloy wheels

Two 15in alloy designs are available. These are the R81 5.5 x 15 seven-hole, which is the standard fitment on the Mini Cooper, and the R82 eight-spoke alloy. Both wheels take a 175/65 R15 tyre, and both are available in silver or white finish, the latter only in conjunction with a white roof.

The R84 X-lite alloy.

16in alloy wheels

The 16in light alloy wheel option is the 6.5 x 16 R83 five-star, available on models with a white roof, in silver or white finish. It is fitted with a 195/55 R16 tyre.

17in alloy wheels

The 17in light alloy wheel is the R85 7 x 17 S-spoke, which comes in silver or white and is fitted with a 205/45 R17 tyre.

No cost options

Just about everything listed above is an extra cost option. Amazingly, however, a number of no cost options are also available. Most of these fall into the 'either/or' category or involve a deletion. They are as follows: eight-spoke alloy wheels on the Mini Cooper in place of the standard seven-hole alloys; five-star alloys on the Cooper S in place of the X-lite wheels; alloy wheels painted in white in conjunction with a white roof on Cooper and Cooper S models; roof and mirror caps in white or black on Cooper and Cooper S, also roof in body colour on these models; model badge deleted (an option which has been available on BMW cars for many years); and, last but not least, to have the interior trim (dashboard and doors etc) in Silver or Anthracite on the Mini Cooper S.

New Mini accessories

In addition to the main optional extras available when purchasing a brand new Mini, a huge range of additional accessories can be obtained from Mini dealers. A number of these accessories are the same as some of the options detailed above, and there is a fair degree of overlap where it is possible and relatively straightforward to add or swap components after the car has been built rather than having to be incorporated at the manufacturing stage. BMW have always produced a very good range of genuine accessories to keep the enthusiastic driver happy and this has been continued into the Mini range. Such accessories also have the advantage of being of the same quality as the rest of the car. Genuine accessories, like sensible factory options, are always a selling point later on as well as being better styled to suit the car from the outset. The complete New Mini accessories list is too long for full details to be

Above right: Additional driving lamps are a popular extra.

Right: The Aero kit for the One and Cooper.

provided here, but the following selection highlights some of the more popular items.

Exterior styling accessories

A lot can be done to further individualise the exterior appearance of a New Mini. Options range from different alloys through to bodykits.

Alloys are an easy way to look different, and are the first extra to consider if you have a Mini One or One D with the standard steel wheels and hubcaps. Alloys really will make a huge difference to these cars. All of the wheels described in the factory options section above are available as accessories. There is also a range of additional wheels which have to be purchased as extras, although when buying a new car it is sometimes possible to work out an arrangement with the dealer if he has an outlet for the standard equipment wheels. It may also be possible to sell the original wheels privately. How easy this is will depend to some extent on the design of the wheels – some are more appealing than others to the private buyer. Alternatively keep the wheels as a spare set!

The available range starts with a 15in alloy, the R86 Star Spoke which is 5.5 x 15. Then in 16in diameter comes the R84 X-lite 6.5 x 16, which is the standard wheel on the Cooper S; the R87 Double Spoke, which is 5.5 x 16; the R88 Double Spoke, a different design and wider at 6.5 x 16; and the R90 Cross Spoke Alloy, which is 6.5 x 16. Moving up to 17in wheels, in addition to the S Spoke listed among the factory options there is the R90 Cross Spoke Composite, which is 7 x 17 and requires 205/45R17V tyres. All of the alloy options set the New Mini off well, the 17in wheels looking particularly good on the Cooper S and all Minis fitted with genuine bodykits. The ride is quite a bit harsher when the 17in wheel options are fitted, due to the very low profile tyres, this being particularly noticeable on Coopers and Cooper S models with Sports Suspension Plus. If comfort is an important consideration then the best ride/appearance compromise is to fit 16in wheels.

Bird's eye view of the Mini roof styling range. (BMW Press)

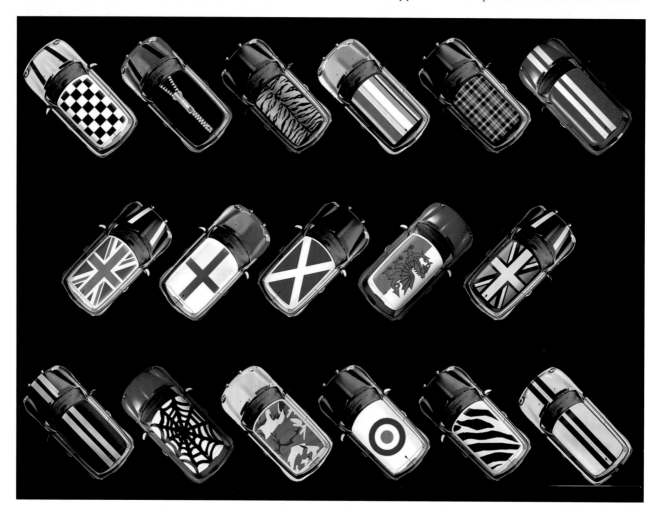

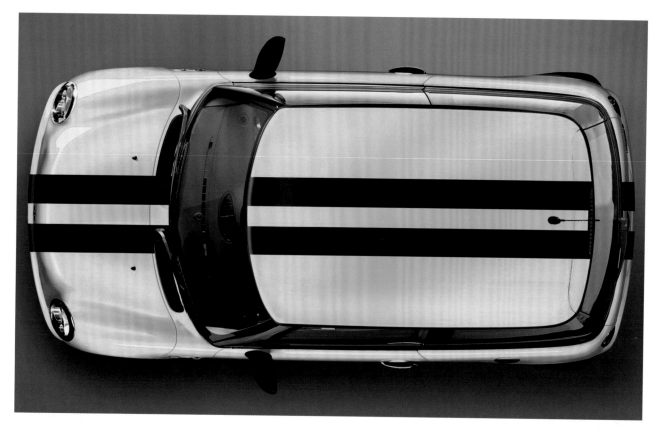

Viper stripes that go over the bonnet, roof, and back of the car.

Lighting accessories come in the form of driving lamps. These are a very traditional addition to the front of a Mini and they featured on the New Minis used in the *Italian Job 2* film. White indicators come as a set complete with side repeaters, high-mounted brake light, and clear-look bulbs. PDC can also be fitted as an accessory (see above for details).

A good way to alter the overall appearance in a somewhat more radical way is to fit the Aerodynamics Package, or 'Aero Kit' as it is generally known. Two types are available, one for the One and Cooper models and one for the Cooper S. The Aero Kit looks good and results in the Mini resembling a John Cooper Challenge race car, but to look at its best on Mini One models it must be fitted in conjunction with Sports Suspension to lower the car slightly. Different versions of the Aero Kit are required for Minis fitted with PDC.

The Cooper and Cooper S come with a white or black roof as standard, and the door mirrors are coloured to match the roof. However, a rather different way of personalising a New Mini is available in the form of numerous roof decal options. Most of the decals are available on black, white, or body colour roofs, but there are some exceptions. The available designs include Target (which consists of red, white, and blue circles), Spider Web, Stars and Stripes (the US flag), Zebra Print, Lion Rampant, St Andrew's Cross, Welsh Flag, Silver Union Jack (available on black roofs only), St George's Cross, Canadian Flag, Chequered Flag, Viper Stripes (available in black, white, or silver), and Union Jack. Roof decals can only be fitted to solid roofs, and are not available with the sunroof option for obvious reasons. The most popular roof decal in the UK and the USA alike is the Union Jack.

If you don't have a factory sliding sunroof then it is possible to fit a fabric folding sunroof. Another highly traditional Mini accessory, this is electrically powered with one-touch operation and two pre-set opening positions.

Mirror covers can be had in chrome as a factory option, and are also available as an accessory, as are chequered exterior mirror covers. The Mini One and Cooper can also have chrome tailpipe trim, or it is possible to go a stage further on these models and fit a sports silencer. The latter is made of stainless steel and produces a sportier exhaust note as well as improving rear end appearance.

The One, One D, and Cooper models can be fitted with a very neat genuine Mini accessory towbar with an unbraked towing capacity of 500kg (1,100lb). With

A rear view of a Mini One with Viper stripes.

Reflecting the British heritage. (BMW Press)

brakes on the trailer, the trailer towing load can be increased to 650kg (1,435lb). This is very useful with a car such as the New Mini which has a very small boot capacity, and using a trailer is also a very good way of ensuring that the rear load area is not subjected to too much wear and tear if dirty or bulky loads are often carried. Unfortunately the towbar cannot be fitted to Cooper S models due to the positioning of the twin centre exit exhaust pipes. If you have a Cooper S or just don't want the hassle of a trailer there are a number of carrying accessories to help. These include bike racks, roof racks, load space protectors, and roof boxes. For the really keen there is even a set of Mini branded luggage to keep everything fully co-ordinated in the boot area.

Another Roof option, the Silver Union Jack (for black roofs only).

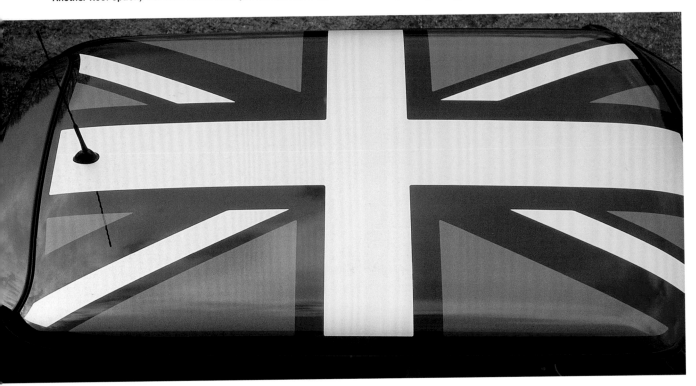

To finish off the exterior and help keep it clean, as well as perhaps reducing the incidence of stone chips, mudflaps can be fitted all round. If you do not have a garage then there are genuine accessory outdoor covers to keep the paintwork in good order and prevent dirt and dust build-up.

Interior accessories

To compliment the exterior upgrades there is an equally large range of equipment to enhance the interior of the car. Floor mats are one of the most worthwhile and important extras for any car, particularly if it is in regular use, as they protect the carpets and maintain them in as new condition. If the mats become dirty or worn they can be replaced easily and inexpensively; the same cannot be said for the carpets. Floor mats can also be fitted to disguise worn carpets where a previous owner has neglected to fit mats in the first place. Three types of mats are available for the New Mini range: Velour mats, which come in Panther Black, Cordoba Beige, Silver Grey, and Lapis Blue; Velour City design mats, which come in Panther Black, Silver Grey, and Cordoba Beige; and harder wearing rubber mats, which are available in front and rear sets in black, beige, grey or red.

There is a range of leather steering wheels, including two-tone versions, as well as leather gear lever knobs and gaiters, Sports seats, and leather upholstery in a variety of colours. Wood interior trim can also be retro

The factory sunroof option.

fitted, as can satellite navigation, albeit a different version to the factory option. The sat nav system is also a high end radio tuner which features RDS and a CD player. Climate control can be fitted to the Mini One and Cooper, and there is a big range of ICE upgrades, including video screens built into the passengers' sun

The sunroof seen from inside the car.

Chrome tailpipe trim. Though this car also has Chrome Line Exterior, it doesn't stand out as much as on darker coloured Minis.

visors and rear seat headrests for watching DVDs. To make the car even cooler there are fold-away sun blinds for the rear window and rear side windows.

Continuing the theme: Mini-branded luggage.

Engine

The only genuine approved engine upgrades for the Mini are the John Cooper Works packages for the Mini Cooper and Cooper S. These are listed in the Mini Accessories brochure – they are, after all, an important optional extra. Full details of these packages are given in Chapter 8.

Ownership and maintenance

Buying a New Mini

Buying a New Mini is an exciting prospect, but there are two very important decisions to be made before rushing out with the chequebook. Firstly, you need to decide which model to go for, and secondly, you have to decide whether to buy that model brand new or used. If buying new there are, as we have seen, five versions to choose from (if the Convertible is considered as one model with three different engine options). Buying used means four options at the time that this book was being put together, since the Convertible was only just becoming available and it is likely to be some time before used examples come onto the market.

The four main New Mini models are readily available used, but the prices of all remain high – there is little depreciation on any of them. For a long time it has been possible to buy a Mini new and not lose very much money when selling a year later. Many people trade up to the next model this way. In the very early days of the New Mini, and the Cooper S in particular, it was even possible to buy one new and sell it at a profit after a few months of use. Although this is no longer likely to be the case it is probable that used prices for all New Mini models will remain strong: they always

The best place to buy a New Mini, new or used, is a Mini dealer. This one is at Long Hanborough in Oxfordshire.

did for the original Mini, and they're still strong for nice examples. Also, BMWs have always retained their values well – even when quite old they hold up well against similar specification and similarly priced (when new) rivals from manufacturers such as Audi or Saab. Overall, then, the prospects for New Minis retaining a relatively high percentage of their value well into old age, whether bought new or used, look very good.

Buying new

The advantages of buying new are, firstly, you know how your car has been treated from day one and, secondly, you'll be able to buy the exact car of your choice in the colour you want and with your own personally chosen optional extras. New Minis are all built to order, so it's not possible to go into a showroom and find a choice of several made to a general spec for sale, as is the case with some cars. It is, needless to say, more expensive to buy new, and a great experience, but for most people whether or not

they do so ultimately comes down to finance. Financing any car is an important consideration. There are many ways of doing this, including bank loans, but in the UK various finance packages are available from Mini dealers. These include Mini Select and Mini Purchase, which are methods of spreading payments to suit individual circumstances and requirements. There are also lease purchase and contract hire packages for the self-employed and business purchasers.

Buying used

Buying used does have one very big advantage: there's no waiting list, as there is for a new Mini. The waiting list for new Minis at the time of writing was in the region of four months, the demand for the New Mini remaining very strong even three years after its introduction and showing no sign of slowing.

Another advantage is that there may be a number of extras on the car, and the cost of these will not be reflected in the used price to anything like the extent that they would be on a new car. The options packs – Salt, Pepper, or Chili – will make some difference, but

More cherished Minis for sale at North Oxford Garage.

the most important extras to look for are air conditioning, either manual or automatic, and items such as alloys on the Mini One and Mini One D. 'Used' does not necessarily mean cheap, though, and there is still occasional evidence of used New Minis selling above the new retail price when people want to avoid that waiting list.

The best way to buy a used New Mini is to purchase it from Mini Cherished, the official BMW-approved used Mini scheme available only from franchised Mini dealers. New Minis offered for sale privately are nearly always cheaper and can be a good deal, but they must be very carefully checked as no warranty will be offered with them.

Which Mini?

It is important to choose the right model for the right reasons. Having said that, whichever New Mini you buy you will enjoy it – none of them are bad, it is simply that some are faster and some more economical than others. All of them are cars that you'll want to drive for pleasure rather than just as a means of getting from A to B. Although the more expensive models in any range of cars are more prestigious than the entry level models this is less pronounced with the New Mini. All New Minis will command a decent amount of respect wherever they go.

Model choice may be dictated by a number of things, especially budget and the age of the driver(s); insurance is difficult for young drivers on any car, and probably close to impossible in the case of a young driver and a Cooper S. For everyday use the Cooper and One are probably best. The Cooper S is quite capable of long everyday journeys but can be slightly less relaxing to drive over long distances, though it more than makes up for this in terms of fun factor. High mileage drivers may wish to take advantage of the economy and low running costs of the frugal Mini One D, which is still good fun to drive due to its high torque, so there is no penalty here. If you require automatic transmission the choice is limited to the One and the Cooper.

Automatic is something well worth considering if commuting in and out of a major city every day where there are high levels of traffic.

New Mini choice summarised

Mini One
* Cheapest to buy
* Economical 90bhp petrol engine giving 42.8mpg combined.
* Five-speed manual transmission or six-speed automatic.
* 0–62 in 10.9 seconds with manual transmission, top speed 112mph.

Mini One D
* Cheapest to run, but only available from June 2003 so less used cars available.
* Very economical 75bhp diesel giving 58.9mpg combined.
* Six-speed manual transmission.
* 0–62 in 13.8 seconds, top speed 103mph.

Mini Cooper
* The most popular New Mini.
* Still economical 115bhp engine giving 41.5mpg combined.
* Five-speed manual transmission or six speed automatic.
* 0–62 in 9.2 seconds, top speed 124mph.

Mini Cooper S
* The quick one.
* Economy not the strongest point, 163bhp and 33.6mpg combined, but most will struggle to achieve the mpg.
* Six-speed manual transmission.
* 0–62 in 7.4 seconds, top speed 135mph.

Mini Convertible
* Great summer fun and open air motoring.
* Choice of engines.
* Unbeatable style.

Areas to check when buying used

Bodywork
The overall condition of the bodywork will give a good indication of how the car has been treated. A lot of small dents and stone chips indicate that the car has had a hard life and the chances are that it hasn't been driven particularly carefully, so mechanical items like the clutch may have been subjected to abuse and increased wear. Minis bought from main dealers or reputable non-franchised outlets will have been properly prepared and any minor body damage repaired, and this is perfectly OK – quality dealers will not buy in an abused car in the first place, as rectification would eat into their profit margin.

When buying, everything that can provide a clue as to how the car has been treated needs to be checked. Floor mats help to protect carpets.

The New Mini will not rust. Plenty of anti-corrosion wax is injected into the cavities at the manufacturing stage.

Fortunately most New Mini owners seem to look after their cars and poor condition examples are rare. One area which is not a problem on the New Mini, unlike its predecessor, is rust. Even three-year-old examples of the previous Mini displayed signs of rust, but this is never likely to be a problem with the New Mini as it is a much better design as far as rusting is concerned. Also the box sections of the body are all wax injected at the factory. BMWs in general have, for some time, had a very good reputation for not rusting – most ten or twelve-year-old E36 3 Series cars, for example, are still completely rust free. Those that do show signs of rusting have usually been badly repaired after an accident. Minis come with a six-year unlimited mileage anti corrosion warranty.

Apart from the condition of the paint the body panels need to be checked for any signs of rippling, and panel fit should be good with very even door, boot, and bonnet gaps. If they are not, suspect poor repairs following accident damage. All plastic trim and chrome work should also be in good condition.

The interior is made of good quality materials and should not show signs of wear and tear. Abused cars may have rattles and loose trim items. Some softening of the leather when fitted, particularly on the driver's seat, may occur, especially on higher mileage cars; check the outer edges of the front seats, especially the driver's side, for scuffing and wear caused by getting in and out of the car. Check, too, the tilting mechanism on the front seats – this has been known to break. One other point to check is that the frameless windows rise and fall as they should when the door is opened and closed.

Engine and transmission

The engines in all New Minis are very reliable units in all states of tune. The normally aspirated petrol engines do sound slightly harsh at high revs when they're being pushed, but this is perfectly normal and is nothing to worry about. The Cooper S engine has a characteristic whine as described in Chapter 6, but this again is perfectly normal and actually sounds quite nice. The gearboxes are all good too, and do not normally show any signs of wear or make unusual noises – if they do, find another car to buy. All manual gearboxes should feel precise and positive. Make sure that the car has a thorough service record and that it comes with Tlc if buying in the UK (see the service section below).

Running gear

Suspension and brakes are reliable on all models, with no commonly known faults. It is important to check that everything is working as it should, with no unusual clunks or noises. Brakes should be very effective and the suspension firm, firmer on Coopers, cars with optional Sports Suspension, and Cooper S models. Premature brake pad wear may be found on very hard driven examples, particularly Cooper Ss. Take a careful look at the condition of the wheels, particularly alloy wheels, and look for signs of damage from kerbing. Replacement wheels are not cheap and damaged rims suggest that the previous owner was a poor driver. Condition of tyres is also important as they are not the cheapest around. Make sure that they are in good condition with no cuts or scrapes, and that they have plenty of tread left. Worn tyres could be a useful bargaining point, though.

Legal stuff

The same rules apply to buying a used New Mini as they do to buying any other car. This is particularly important when buying privately or from a non-franchised dealer. It is very important to check the identity of the car. The registration document should have the seller's correct name and address, and it is worth checking past MoT certificates and the service history to verify the mileage and that the car is genuine. Telephone the dealer who has serviced the car to verify mileage and that the service record is indeed genuine.

To avoid buying a car with a hidden history it is worth having it checked. This will help to ensure that it hasn't been recorded as an insurance write off, been involved in a major accident, or stolen, and that it has no outstanding finance on it. This is particularly important with a recent model car like the New Mini. In the UK this means calling the AA or HPI who will, for a fee, check the vehicle for you and offer a guarantee against many of the above-mentioned problems before you buy.

Maintaining a New Mini
Servicing and repair

The timing of service intervals on the New Mini is determined by the car's electronic system. The information is displayed on a service level indicator, so there is no excuse for anyone forgetting to have the car serviced. Mileages between services will vary to quite a degree according to the type of use, driving conditions, and the driving style of the owner, but generally speaking the first service will be required between 10,000 and 12,500 miles, with subsequent services required every 15,000 to 20,000 miles.

Tlc

UK customers for brand-new Minis can opt to purchase Mini Tlc. For a one-off charge (£100 at the time of writing) scheduled servicing is covered for up to five years or 50,000 miles. Tlc is available to both fleet and private customers and represents outstanding value. As

The seat tilting memory system has been known to fail. Check carefully.

a result very few if any New Minis are bought without it. Tlc is transferable to the new owner if the car is sold during the contract period, so a customer buying a three-year-old Mini with Tlc will still have two years of free servicing. This is another reason why the price of used Minis remains strong. New Minis without the Tlc package should be avoided.

The Tlc service schedule is as follows:

Oil Service
Body/electrics
* Heating/air conditioning system: renew micro filter.

Engine compartment
* Change engine oil and renew filter element.
* Reset service indicator in accordance with manufacturer's directives.

Running gear
* Brake pads: measure thickness with measuring gauge. If brake pads renewed, clean brake caliper gaps.
* Brake discs: check surface and thickness.
* Alloy wheels: grease wheel centring surfaces.
* Parking brake: check functioning and adjust as necessary. Repair according to manufacturer's instructions.

Mini servicing is very thorough. Here a technician is checking the controls.

Inspection 1
Body/electrics
* Check the lights.
* Check the instrument and display lighting and the heater blower.
* Check the horn, headlight flasher, and hazard warning flashers.
* Seat belts: check condition of belts, and function of reels, belt locks, and belt catches.
* Battery: check battery charge. If necessary recharge battery.
* Heating/air conditioning system: renew micro filter.
* If the car is equipped with Mini Mobility System it is important that you change the sealant bottle after four years.
* Inspect the entire body except cavities for corrosion.

Engine compartment
* Brief diagnostic test.
* Change engine oil and renew filter element.
* Check coolant level. When refilling check concentration. Change the coolant after a maximum of four years (filling quantity as required).
* Reset service indicator in accordance with manufacturer's directives.
* Windscreen (and headlight cleaning system if appropriate): check fluid level and top up if necessary.
* Power steering reservoir: check oil level. Add oil if necessary.
* Brake fluid: renew according to service interval indicator display, but not later than after two years.

Running gear

* Brake pads: measure thickness with measuring gauge. If brake pads renewed, clean brake caliper gaps.
* Brake discs: check surface and thickness.
* Alloy wheels: grease wheel centring surfaces.
* Steering components: check for freedom from play, leaks, wear, and damage.
* Underbody including all visible parts: check for damage, leaks, and corrosion.
* Parking brake: check functioning and adjust as necessary. Repair according to manufacturer's instructions.
* Tyres: check pressures and correct if necessary (including spare wheel), then initialise run-flat indicator. Check external condition, tread depth, and tread wear pattern.

Final check

* Test drive to check roadworthiness.
* Bed down brakes.
* Check steering or power steering.
* Check clutch.
* Check shock absorbers (visual examination).
* Check telltale.
* Check Control.

Inspection 2

Inspection 2 is the big service. Much of its content is the same as Inspection 1, but with additional items. As with the Oil Service and Inspection 1, the full service is listed here.

Body/electrics

* Check the lights.
* Check the instrument and display lighting and the heater blower.
* Check the horn, headlight flasher, and hazard warning flashers.
* Seat belts: check condition of belts, and function of reels, belt locks, and belt catches.
* Battery: check battery charge. If necessary recharge battery.
* Heating/air conditioning system: renew micro filter.
* If the car is equipped with Mini Mobility System it is important that you change the sealant bottle after four years.
* Inspect the entire body except cavities for corrosion.

Engine compartment

* Brief diagnostic test.
* Change engine oil and renew filter element.
* Check coolant level. When refilling check concentration. Change the coolant after a maximum of four years (filling quantity as required).
* Reset service indicator in accordance with manufacturer's directives.
* Windscreen (and headlight cleaning system if appropriate): check fluid level and top up if necessary.
* Power steering reservoir: check oil level. Add oil if necessary.
* Brake fluid: renew according to service interval indicator display, but not later than after two years.

Downloading and transmitting any fault codes to the central computer.

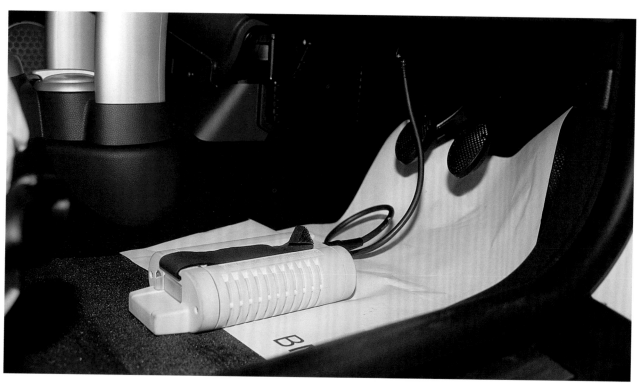

Above: Checking the tyres and wheel rims for damage.

Left: Particular attention is paid to the steering, suspension, and brakes.

* Renew the spark plugs.
* Intake air silencer: renew air cleaner element (renew more frequently in very dusty conditions).
* Renew poly-V belt.

Running gear
* Brake pads: measure thickness with measuring gauge. If brake pads renewed, clean brake caliper gaps.
* Brake discs: check surface and thickness.
* Alloy wheels: grease wheel centring surfaces.
* Steering components: check for freedom from play, leaks, wear, and damage.
* Underbody including all visible parts: check for damage, leaks, and corrosion.
* Parking brake: check functioning and adjust as necessary. Repair according to manufacturer's instructions.
* Tyres: check pressures and correct if necessary (including spare wheel), then initialise run-flat indicator. Check external condition, tread depth, and tread wear pattern.

Right: A thorough check is made of all underside components both front and rear. This is the underside of a Mini Cooper.

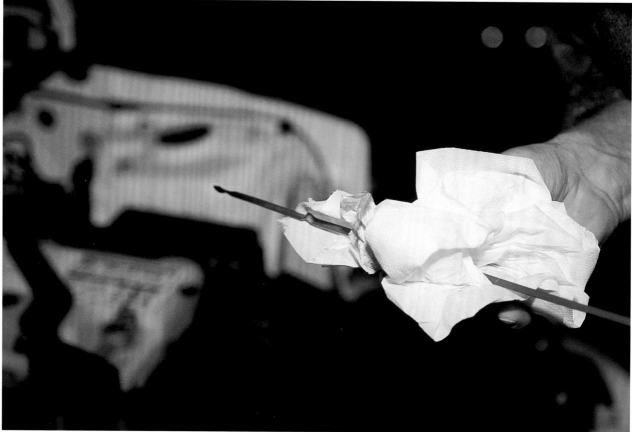

Left: Undoing the oil drain plug under the car.

Below left: Checking the engine oil level.

Final check

* Test drive to check roadworthiness.
* Bed down brakes.
* Check steering or power steering.
* Check clutch.
* Check shock absorbers (visual examination).
* Check telltale.
* Check Control.

With all of the above services, if items such as the brake pads need renewing or the parking brake requires adjustment this is charged in addition to the flat rate for the service. Working through the above listings shows the value of the Tlc package. BMW servicing which is the same as Mini servicing by Mini dealers is very thorough. Everything is fully checked and any problems brought to the attention of the customer. This is also reassuring for UK owners when it comes to MoT test time, since if the car has been serviced by a Mini dealer the chances are that any problems will have been rectified as they occurred, and the car will sail through the test without problem. Even after Tlc has expired it is well worth continuing to have your New Mini serviced by a franchised Mini dealer, as this will maintain the service record correctly and really will make a difference to the value of the car all through its life. It certainly does with older BMWs: those without a proper service record are worth considerably less and are much harder to sell.

Owner maintenance

Today, a lot of servicing work cannot be carried out by a home mechanic. This is increasingly becoming the case with all cars as the role of electronic and computer controlled systems grows. With Tlc in the UK there is absolutely no need for any home servicing for the first five years anyway. However, there are a number of checks that should be made at home on a regular basis to keep a New Mini running at its best between services. These include checking tyre pressures and the condition of the wheels, especially if they are alloy, and checking the oil level, the brake and clutch fluid levels, and the engine oil level. A general check should be kept on all other components including the bodywork so that any problems can be rectified quickly.

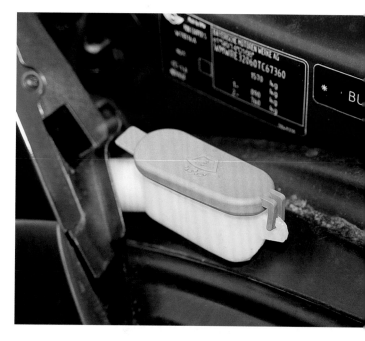

The screen and headlamp washer fill-up points are either side of the car under the bonnet at the top of the wheel arch.

Bodywork maintenance

Regular cleaning of the bodywork is essential to maintain a New Mini in top condition. Polishing every three to six months (depending upon how often and where the car is used) will make a considerable

Checking the power steering fluid level.

Location of the cooling system filler.

on alloys will cause them to rapidly deteriorate. Washing them weekly will go a long way towards slowing down this deterioration and will also have the benefit of making the whole car look reasonably clean even when the rest of the body is slightly dirty.

Small scratches and scuffs on the body can often be removed with a scratch removing compound. It will usually be necessary to polish the whole panel afterwards to restore shine. Stone chips and larger scratches should be touched in quickly to prevent rusting. If you do not feel confident about doing this some BMW dealers have a minor bodywork clinic to repair scratches and to remove small dents without having to repaint the panel. Provided that they are not too bad alloy wheel chips and scuffs can also be repaired. There are also a number of mobile companies who specialise in this type of repair. Ask your Mini dealer to recommend one to ensure that any repairs you have done are to a high standard.

Storing a New Mini

Although the New Mini is well protected against rust it is always a good idea to garage it whenever this is possible. Sometimes it isn't. Many people don't have a garage or it is full of other items, or another car, in which case an excellent alternative is a car cover. Car covers are available as genuine Mini accessories, or there are a number of alternatives on the market. Outdoor covers such as the one made by Cover Systems are inexpensive and will keep your car clean and free from dust and tree sap. Good covers are breathable to allow the car to dry out quickly, though this does mean that they let some water through when it rains. It also means that condensation, which always forms under the cover, will also dry out quickly. A cover is particularly useful when the car is not in use every day.

Mini clubs

Apart from maintaining and driving and adding accessories to your New Mini there is another way to get more out of it. Today there are literally hundreds of Mini clubs throughout the world, and the vast majority welcome owners of New Minis as much as they do owners of the original cars. Indeed, many members of Mini clubs own one or more of both new and old Minis, and there are also some clubs specifically for the New Mini. There is always plenty of help and advice available and a great many social, and in some cases even some competitive, events throughout the year.

difference too. A range of polishes is available from BMW and some really excellent aftermarket polishes are available too. Find one that is right for you and your car and use it regularly.

A New Mini is not a large car and can be maintained in top condition with relatively little time spent on it, although keeping it looking its best is not a chore and can be just as pleasurable as driving it. For a quick spruce up a car wash shampoo that includes wax polish can work wonders, although the car will need to be rinsed fully and leathered off to prevent streaking as it dries. If the Mini is in daily use a weekly wash is going to be required. If it is not possible to wash the whole car at least try to wash the wheels. This is very important if alloys are fitted, since leaving brake dust

Chapter **Eleven**

Tuning and modification

Very soon after the launch of the original Mini enthusiasts began to realise its potential, mainly due to the fact that it handled so well. If it could be made to go very fast too, it would really be something to be reckoned with. Consequently when the 997cc Mini Cooper arrived at the end of 1961 a huge Mini tuning and accessory market began. That market has grown ever since, and is probably as big today as it has ever been. With this history behind it, the New Mini obviously had to follow suit. It already had fantastic handling and the Cooper S was no slouch to start with, but there was room for more in virtually all areas. BMW themselves were very aware of this, and produce a large range of accessories as well as having the John Cooper Works engine upgrades that we have looked at in earlier chapters.

Many owners have opted for JCW conversions during the early years of the New Mini because these retain the Mini three-year warranty. However, some owners are not bothered about the warranty and, with this in mind and an eye to the future, several independent tuners have produced some interesting alternatives, meaning that a number of performance upgrades are already available, along with a lot of performance parts to tune the brakes and suspension, plus numerous dress-up parts and accessories. It is likely that this alternative market will expand considerably as New Minis start to age, and all the signs are in place that the New Mini tuning market may very well end up larger than that of the original car. Certainly it is likely to become larger in money terms quite quickly, as upgrade components for the new model are a lot more expensive and much more in line with tuning parts for other more modern cars.

Tuned New Minis have been produced by some of the traditional BMW tuning companies and some of the

traditional Mini tuners. A lot of development work has gone into performance upgrades of all models from the Mini One upwards, with, perhaps not surprisingly, the bulk of the work being concentrated on the Cooper S. It's impossible to cover all of the tuners or all the packages on offer in just one chapter of a book, so what follows is really no more than a taster of what's available. Comprehensive details can be found in the *New Mini Performance Manual*, which is also to be published by Haynes.

Tuned New Minis

One of the first performance upgrades for the Cooper S was produced by Hartge, renowned BMW tuners for many years. Development of this engine upgrade started as soon as the S was launched. Although not BMW backed like the JCW upgrades, this conversion is close to home and most BMW dealers (95 per cent according to Birds, who are the UK Hartge agents) will service the Hartge S under Tlc. Having said this, if considering this conversion or any other modification from any supplier it is absolutely essential to check with your Mini dealer first!

The Hartge conversion is a 210bhp upgrade based around modifications to the supercharger and drive assemblies with revised engine management settings, and each modified car is individually mapped. The new engine management maps for UK customers are

DID YOU KNOW?

The original Mini must be the most tuned and modified car of all time, but with the huge range of tuning and performance parts that are coming onto the market almost daily the New Mini may eventually overtake it.

programmed and transmitted from Hartge's studios near Merzig in Germany. German customers can have their cars converted and mapped on site. The conversion has TuV approval at 200bhp, although the Birds dyno figures are 210bhp and figures of 212–215bhp have been achieved in Germany. On the road this translates into a 0–60 time of 6.6 seconds and a top speed of 144mph. Hartge conversions are subjected to a number of endurance tests before being released. Hartge also produce a software upgrade for the Mini One which is designed to increase the performance of the standard engine to just above that of the standard Mini Cooper.

Another conversion that is close to BMW is the

at any given engine speed. As a result boost is up, which, together with a modified exhaust system, increases power to 193bhp at 7,000rpm, giving a quoted 0–62 time of 7.0 seconds and a top speed of 145mph.

A well-known UK-based BMW tuner is Ray West. An ex-touring car driver, Ray has produced some interesting supercharged BMWs in the past and has now turned his hand to tuning the Cooper S. The West Tuning S is more powerful than some other conversions and a greater number of modifications are carried out to the engine. The bottom end of the Pentagon engine is very robust – all tuners agree on this point – so it has been left as standard on the West Mini. The cylinder head has been extensively modified, being fully gas flowed with opened up ports and larger inlet and exhaust valves. An uprated camshaft is also fitted, to increase valve lift and duration. On the fuelling side there is a larger throttle body and the exhaust is replaced with a bigger bore item. Also a new catalyst is fitted which is much freer flowing. Modifications are made to the ECU to provide more fuel all through the range.

West Tuning say this combination of modifications produces 243bhp. The improvement is certainly noticeable in the performance figures, which are down to under six seconds to 60 and a top speed in excess of 150mph. To cope with the extra performance modifications have been made to the suspension in the form of Leda dampers and springs, which lower the car by 30mm as well as stiffening it slightly. The brakes are upgraded too, with special West Tuning 308mm diameter vented front discs and AP Racing four pot 5000 series calipers.

A company that has been tuning original Minis for many years is Mini Sport in Padiham, Lancashire. Mini Sport have carried out a lot of development work on the New Mini and offer a number of packages to improve performance, all of which have been extensively researched and developed in-house by their team of engineers and road testers.

Beginning with the Mini One there is the Phase 1 Tuning Kit, which is an entry level package designed to increase driveability and performance. The kit includes an engine management upgrade, a K&N sport induction air filter kit, and a stainless steel exhaust system. This upgrade provides a 30bhp gain on the Mini One and a 15bhp increase on the Mini Cooper. Next up is the

upgrade produced by AC Schnitzer. Again, this is an upgrade for the Cooper S and is available from some BMW dealers, as BMW GB are UK distributors of AC Schnitzer products. Alternatively it can be obtained direct from AC Schnitzer in Germany. This conversion is also a revised supercharger drive system, which drives the supercharger faster than the standard component

Phase 2 Tuning Kit, which gives an extra 55bhp to the Mini One and 30bhp to the Cooper. This kit again modifies the engine management system and also includes a performance cylinder head, performance camshaft, stainless steel manifold, and stainless steel full exhaust system. There is also a sports catalytic converter and twin silencers.

Mini Sport offer four levels of tune for the Mini Cooper S. The S/E Phase 1 Tuning Kit is a 200bhp conversion which tunes the supercharger and engine for maximum mid-range punch. This is followed by the S/E Phase 2 Tuning Kit giving 220bhp, which in addition to the components in the 200bhp kit also includes a water-to-air chargecooler to ensure air entering the engine is as cold and dense as possible. The new chargecooler sits in place of the original intercooler and is extremely straightforward to fit with minimum modifications.

Moving on up the scale, the 235bhp conversion is as the 220bhp kit with the addition of the uprated Mini Sport S/E camshaft which Mini Sport say provides the S with more usable power and torque whilst retaining its drivability. There is also an S/E twin exit exhaust system and an S/E high flow exhaust manifold which significantly increases the outflow of the exhaust gases from the engine. The S/E twin exit stainless steel exhaust is unusual, as the sound level is variable according to the owner's wishes. This is made possible by easily accessed removable DD deadeners in the rear silencers.

The S/E Phase 4 Tuning Kit is the ultimate Mini Sport conversion and produces 250bhp. The content is as per the 235bhp conversion but with the addition of a big valve cylinder head. Mini Sport say that in developing this head they've applied everything they've learned from nearly 40 years of preparing original competition Minis together with the latest flow-bench techniques. The combustion chambers are individually shaped and balanced before being polished. The heads come equipped with uprated valves and guides, as well as valve springs and stem seals.

A vast range of tuning equipment and complete packages are also available from Minispeed. Based in the South of England, Minispeed are well known for tuning and building all versions of the original Mini and, like Mini Sport (who are based in the North), have their own workshops and a rolling road for the fitting and setting up of uprated components. Minispeed have also carried out a great deal of development work, which has been done in conjunction with a number of important tuning component manufacturers. Starting with the Mini One, the first stage is an ECU remap which will increase power from 90bhp up to 115bhp as per the Mini Cooper. This is a relatively inexpensive conversion. For those seeking to improve on the Cooper output, the Mini One can be taken to 130bhp with the Stage 2 package, which consists of further remapping of the ECU. Next up is the Stage 3 conversion. This includes a remap plus a big valve cylinder head, a fast road cam, an induction kit, and a stainless steel performance exhaust system. This moves the power output up to 150bhp. The ultimate Minispeed kit for the One is the Stage 4, which includes all of the upgrades contained in the Stage 3 kit plus a stainless steel tubular exhaust manifold and a bespoke inlet manifold. Minispeed probably do more for the Mini One than any other tuner, which is excellent news for anyone starting off with a One and wishing to upgrade in stages rather than selling up in order to get a Cooper.

The Minispeed Cooper tuning packages come in three levels and are similar to those offered for the One, the Cooper Stage 1 being an inexpensive remap to increase power from 115 up to 130bhp. Stage 2 comprises an ECU remap, a big valve cylinder head, fast road cam, induction kit, and a stainless steel exhaust system, and increases the power output to 150bhp. The ultimate Minispeed Cooper conversion is the Stage 3, which consists of the Stage 2 kit plus a stainless steel tubular exhaust manifold and the bespoke inlet manifold. It produces 165bhp.

Minispeed also have plenty to offer for the Cooper S. Five stages of tune are available, beginning with Stage 1, which is an ECU remap and a smaller supercharger pulley which will up the power from 163bhp to 195. Stage 2 includes the upgrades in Stage 1 plus an induction kit, a raised rev limit, and a modified supercharger, the result being 215bhp. Stage 3 is as Stage 2 plus a Minispeed uprated camshaft giving another 10bhp and bringing the output up to 225bhp. Stage 4 involves the addition of a big valve head and stainless steel tubular exhaust manifold, giving 245bhp. The final package, Stage 5, includes a large top mount intercooler with water spray, a modified throttle body,

DID YOU KNOW?

The tuneability of the New Mini engine is ultimately limited by the cylinder head design, as the spark plug tubes prevent very high lift camshafts from being fitted.

Most of the big names in Mini tuning have modified New Minis. This is the Mini Spares Cooper displaying white Cooper bonnet stripes.

and a modified inlet manifold. Minispeed say this combination produces in excess of 260bhp, which represents an increase of around 100bhp over standard. With power levels this high attention must also be paid to the suspension and brakes.

Minispeed also offer a power boost for the Mini One D. This provides a 21 per cent power increase and an 18 per cent increase in torque.

A number of performance kits for the Cooper S are available from Mini Spares in conjunction with AmD. There are five stages: Stage 1 (200–210bhp), which concentrates on supercharger mods; Stage 2 (220bhp) adds a Milltek exhaust manifold and system with performance cat; Stage 3 (230bhp) has in addition an induction kit and larger throttle body; Stage 4 (240bhp) adds a gas flowed cylinder head; and Stage 5 (255bhp) adds a gas flowed big valve cylinder head and lightened flywheel. All conversions are set up on the rolling road at AmD's premises at Bicester near Oxford. AmD also produce upgrades for the Mini One and Cooper.

These are just some of the many conversions available world-wide for the New Mini. As with all tuning conversions similar lines of thought run through most of them, but there are also a number of

interesting differences in both the modified parts and the power output figures. All the companies mentioned above are reputable and all the figures quoted (which come from the tuning companies themselves) were obtained on a rolling road. However, they were not all obtained on the same rolling road and this should be taken into consideration when comparing them – most rolling roads produce slightly different figures. The cars were not tested independently for this book.

Performance and tuning equipment
Engine

The Mini conversions detailed above are complete packages, and although some of them can be bought as a kit of parts for home fitting, in reality the vast majority of people will have the conversions fitted by a specialist. This makes sense, as many require rolling road tuning and remapping which cannot be carried out at home. However, for anyone wishing to build their own engine lots of tuning components are also available as parts from a number of companies.

Building a high performance New Mini engine is simpler than for many other cars, and certainly considerably simpler than the old Mini ever was because the bottom end of the engine doesn't need any modification, being strong enough in standard form. This means that engines can on the whole be modified in situ without having to be removed from the car. Should it be necessary, though, engine removal is not actually difficult as the front end of the car removes quite easily (see the section on building a Cooper S Works in Chapter 8), allowing excellent access to virtually everything.

Modified cylinder heads are available from several suppliers. Most first stage heads are fully ported and polished but retain standard valves. More power can be obtained with the next stage of head, which is also fitted with larger inlet and exhaust valves. Both types of head are available for the One/Cooper and the Cooper S. Performance fast road camshafts giving increased lift and duration can also be obtained. Again these are available for both normally aspirated petrol-engined Minis and the supercharged S. There is not a great deal of choice of cam available as yet but it is early days, and it seems likely that a greater range will be developed in time.

Big gains can be made by changing the supercharger pulley, to make the supercharger spin faster and thus increase boost pressure. Two types of pulley are available, a press-on type and a bolt-on type. A special tool is required to remove the pulley. Although this can be purchased from specialists such as Minispeed, the pulley is fitted on incredibly tightly and many people will prefer to let an expert change theirs.

An important supercharger related mod is an upgraded intercooler. A number of possibilities have been tried and the most effective and practical so far is to fit an increased capacity unit in the standard position on top of the supercharger. A larger intercooler provides a 40 per cent increase in cooling area and has the added advantage of not requiring any modifications to the car or supercharger to fit. The rolling road power figures are very different on the same car when cool air is entering the supercharger. The temperature of the incoming air is very important, particularly on supercharged cars, so this is a modification that should prove very worthwhile. In particular this mod plays an important part in the power increase between Stages 4 and 5 of the Minispeed conversions for the Cooper S described above. The Minispeed cooler also comes with a water spray kit which further increases efficiency.

A very popular and easy-to-fit mod is a freeflow air filter. These are available as replacement elements and as induction kits from most New Mini specialists and are made by a number of manufacturers, including K&N, Pipercross, and Green. Some air filter kits are better than others – some will give a 1–2bhp increase, others none – so take advice and buy carefully. A ram air induction system manufactured by Gruppe M, who supply Formula One teams, is available from Birds. Intended for fast road and track day applications, it is designed to produce accelerated airflow into the engine and Birds say it will produce an extra 12bhp between 5,800 and 6,800rpm.

The gearboxes fitted to the New Mini range are more than adequate for the job and can take reasonable levels of power increase. The Rover-derived gearbox fitted to the One and Cooper up until July 2004 will not cope with huge power increases. For very highly tuned Coopers and Ones a straight cut five-speed gearbox conversion is available. A limited slip differential can also be fitted to the straight cut gearbox. The six-speed Getrag gearbox on the Mini Cooper S is a lot stronger and is not known for causing problems when the engine is tuned for high outputs. A Quaife limited slip diff is available for fitment to the Cooper S. A quickshift gearchange can also be fitted to all manual gearboxes to create a racier gearchange with shorter throw.

The exhaust system

Changing the standard exhaust system on all of the petrol-engined Minis makes a big improvement, as it does on many cars. This is proved by the fact that an improved exhaust features in all of the conversions (excluding the pure remaps) described earlier in this chapter. A number of exhaust upgrade options are available from several companies. Play Mini – who are very well known in the Japanese market for a large range of Mini parts and accessories and also well

Engine removal on a New Mini for major rebuilds is actually fairly straightforward.

known in the UK for original Mini exhausts – produce systems for the Mini One and Cooper consisting of a 3in slashcut rear silencer or TT style rear silencer and a link pipe. A Cooper S system is also available, and a stainless steel tubular exhaust manifold including a performance cat to fit all models. Play Mini systems are all made from stainless steel.

A stainless steel high performance exhaust manifold and catalyst upgrade is also produced by Milltek. This four-into-one system, with substantially lengthened primary pipes, considerably improves the outflow of the exhaust gases. In addition the cat is much improved over standard, containing a 250 cell per inch metal catalyst which offers a 34 per cent greater open area than the standard catalyst and reduces back pressure. It is unaffected by prolonged exposure to the high temperatures of the exhaust system. When coupled to a Milltek exhaust system the Milltek manifold and cat will give an 18bhp power increase. This system is available from Minispeed, Moss, and Birds, who also sell Hartge sports exhausts. Two sports silencers are available for the Cooper S, a twin 72mm central pipe system or a four outlet system. Four pipes on a small car like the Mini often looks overcrowded, but this system, reminiscent of the BMW E46 M3, does look very good. Scorpion also produce stainless systems, a slashcut tailpipe system for the One and Cooper and a twin tailpipe system for the S.

Suspension

New Mini suspension can be upgraded over the standard factory product by fitting components from several of the well known spring and damper manufacturers. Many people will be content with the factory upgrades of Sports Suspension and Sports Suspension Plus at the lower levels of tune, but for the very serious upgrades, particularly on the Cooper S, further lowered and stiffened suspension will be of benefit. Upgrade units are available from Leda, Spax, Gaz, and Bilstein. Most systems are fully adjustable for both height and stiffness and will lower the car by up to 30mm (Gaz) or 40mm (Bilstein).

It is important to select the correct kit, which is the one best suited to driving conditions and your driving style. The Spax kit, for instance, allows lowering of between 15 and 50mm and is adjustable on the car, making it ideal for track days and road use. Many of the other systems offer similar adjustments. Lowering springs are made by Apex, and suspension kits are also sold by John Cooper Works and Birds (Hartge).

Uprating Mini suspension eliminates the pitching which can be experienced and also the light feeling that can occur at high speeds and under very fast acceleration. Stiffening the suspension will have a slightly detrimental effect on ride quality, as will lowering – the New Mini is already low in standard form, particularly the Sports Suspension equipped cars, and further lowering can make ground clearance a problem on the road over potholes and speed bumps. Although it looks good, it is wise to beware of going too low.

The bodyshell is already very stiff in construction, but for very fast road use or competition use a front strut brace offers additional rigidity.

Another mod is to fit upgraded rear suspension control arms. The standard arms can be prone to

Twin tailpipes with a difference. These are on a Cooper.

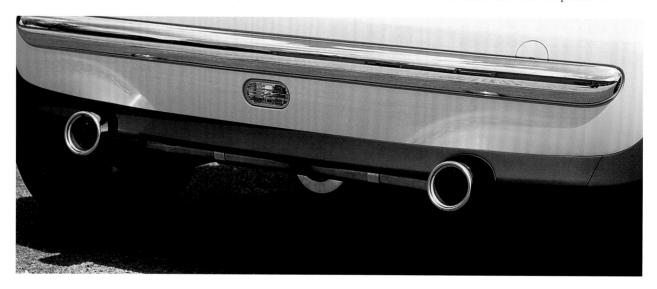

A Hartge-modified Cooper S. (Birds)

Lowered suspension looks fantastic on a New Mini. This car has been lowered for racing, and is too low for the road under most circumstances.

flexing, and stronger arms will give a more solid feel. Fixed chromoly arms are available from Moss and adjustable alloy arms from Minispeed.

Another suspension upgrade which will appeal to some but not others is to fit Powerflex suspension bushes. These are polyurethane replacement bushes to replace the standard rubber items. They are 25–30 per cent stiffer and give increased control over the handling at the expense of a very slight increase in harshness. They are also available for the steering rack mounts, the bump stops, and the engine mountings.

Performance tyres will have an effect upon handling. Good tyres are made by Yokohama, the A539 coming in 205/50 x 16, 205/45 x 17, and 205/40 x 17. Birds fit Pirelli P7000 215/35 x 18 tyres to the 7.5 x 18 Hartge rims on their cars and numerous testers have reported a marked improvement in both handling and ride comfort over the standard run-flat tyres.

Brakes

Brakes can be upgraded by fitting grooved and cross drilled front and rear brake discs or EBC Turbo grooved discs and EBC Greenstuff upgraded pads all round. This will improve the brakes sufficiently for most road applications, but for ultimate stopping power with some of the most powerful engine conversions there is

the AP Racing big brake kit. This consists of cross drilled 304 x 24mm 40 vane discs with four pot calipers, a set of fast road or race pads, braided hoses, and all fittings and fasteners, plus some DOT 5.1 brake fluid. The calipers have dust seals, anti rattle clips for the pads, and a durable anti-corrosion finish, making them suitable for everyday road use. Birds offer a Sports front brake kit with a 328 x 28mm floating set of front discs complete with 7075 T-6 billet aluminium mounting bells, a pair of ST 40 four piston calipers, and stainless steel brake liners. These are very big brakes and require 17 or 18in wheels. With all big brake conversions check wheel clearance before buying and fitting.

Some aftermarket alloys look good. This is the Mini Spares Mini with TSW alloys.

Variations on a theme, another Hartge S. (Birds)

Wheels

If the factory options range of alloy wheels is not enough then there are numerous aftermarket alternatives to choose from, including some exceptionally nice designs. Particularly worthy of note are those produced by Minilite, who supplied the alloys for the original BMC Works rally Minis back in the 1960s and early 1970s. The 7 x 16in wheel for the New Mini has been produced to celebrate Minilite's 40th year in wheel manufacturing, and will fit all models in

the range. Other very nice wheels are made by Hartge. These are larger diameter 18in wheels and come in two designs, the Classic and a special Union Jack design. Another company which produces a stylish alloy wheel is Hamann Motorsport, a well known German company which manufactures a number of upgrade components for BMW. This is a five-spoke design in silver with a polished outer rim and is available in 17 and 18in diameters. Eighteen-inch diameter wheels are the largest that should be fitted to a New Mini, and even then minor wheel arch modification will probably be necessary to accommodate certain designs. Some people have fitted 19in wheels, but there will definitely be wheel arch rubbing problems with these; they also look far too big on a car the size of a Mini.

Another very good range of wheels is the Image three-piece split rims. There are several styles and each design is available in a number of sizes. There are many other wheels, far too many to detail here. For individual choice it is best to visit one of the larger New Mini specialists.

A locking wheel nut kit is essential if expensive alloys are fitted. These are available from Mini and from most specialists and provide increased peace of mind for owner and insurance companies alike.

Huge wheels such as these 19in examples look too big. Wheel arch clearance problems are also likely.

18in wheels are as far as you should go. These are Birds Union Jack alloys. (Birds)

Many owners choose to colour code their Minis for a cleaner look.

The wheel arches do blend in better with the rest of the car when given this treatment.

Styling accessories

There is a massive amount of styling equipment available for the New Mini. The Aero bodykit is very popular and looks good. A further tweak which can be carried out with or without the kit is to colour code the wheel arch trims. This can be done by a Mini dealer or a competent paintshop.

Alternative exterior styling kits are made by Hamann. These include a front spoiler for the Mini One and Cooper, a spoiler for the Cooper S, and a rear apron to suit the twin central exhaust of the S. Hamann also make a rear roof spoiler which fits on the tailgate but is a slightly different design to the BMW item. Zeemax make full bodykits, and two designs of wheel arch extensions are available from Mini Spares – narrow arches with front and lower lips or huge arches with a bodykit.

There are many more smaller dress-up parts, such as chrome side repeater vents, clear light lenses and additional front driving lamps, and a four lamp works spot lamp kit with a stainless steel lamp bar. Clear headlamp protectors are a good idea. These are made of soft material to absorb the impact from stones and gravel – an inexpensive way to protect the headlamps, but only available for lights without washers. For a different look to mirror covers that are in white or black there are mirror gloves made of stitched vinyl, giving a touch of the vintage look.

Mini Spares offer a Cooper S fuel cap conversion for non S models which uses genuine Mini parts and works with the central locking.

There is also plenty to choose from for the interior. There are chrome bezels for instrument vents and gear lever, billet door sill plates, and a vast range of gear knobs and different pedals and foot rests. Aftermarket floor mats change the look slightly, as does a dashboard mat which conforms to the contours of the top of the dash.

For a totally different interior look there is Newton

Above right: Sill finishers remove easily for this.

Right: The Aero kit, fitted to a lot of modified cars.

Below: All bodykits require the removal of the front and rear bumpers.

Popular addition, the Newton Commercial centre armrest.

A quality alternative to leather, again from Newton Commercial. Good for converting cloth-trimmed Minis.

Commercial's collection. Newton are British Motor Heritage approved, and their product range includes leather seat covers supplied with new foam cushions for fitting to the original New Mini seat frames. Fitting can be carried out at home or, preferably, entrusted to a competent trim shop or a Mini dealer. The covers have been tested by MIRA (the Motor Industry Research Association) and conform to the Air Bag Worthiness certificate. The seat covers are available in several modern designs or the original brocade pattern from the Mark One Mini Cooper and S of the 1960s. The quality is excellent, and this follows through to the centre console armrests, handbrake grips, leather steering wheels, and footwell carpets also offered by the company.

The finishing interior touch for those who like plenty of in-car entertainment is designed for cars with the factory satellite navigation option. Birds offer a Mini Mobile Media package which adds television and a Playstation to the central screen. In Japan customers get this as standard with the sat nav system.

New Mini
in competition

The words Mini and motorsport belong together. The original Mini must have been used in competition more than any other single type of car in the history of motoring. In the 1960s and 1970s many Minis were used as daily transport to and from work, and for the school run, but at the weekend participated in club level competitions of some sort. Minis have been entered into just about every type of motorsport going, and they have been very successful at it, with the low costs involved enabling many individuals to take part. The BMC Works rally team and the Cooper Works racing team were renowned for their successes.

A racing New Mini undergoing preparation.

The New Mini has excellent handling and has so far proved itself to be a very tuneable car with a chassis capable of coping with large increases in power. Although still very new it is already beginning to make its mark as a competition car, and a number have been

The JCW alloys and race lowered suspension.

privately entered in various events world-wide. The New Mini certainly has the breeding, from both its BMC/BL/Rover and BMW backgrounds. Over the next few years more cars are likely to be entered in competitions, and more championship events will start to appear. The original Mini has had its own one-model race championships (in the form of Mini Se7en racing and Mini Miglia) for many years, and this is still going strong. The New Mini is following in these same footsteps, with its own race series – the John Cooper Challenge – which is now well established in the UK. On the rallying front a new championship event was announced by Mini Sport as this book was going to press.

Racing

The John Cooper Challenge

One-make racing is always very exciting for competitors and spectators alike, as the cars are all built to the same specification and driver skill plays an even more important role than in racing where a number of different makes and models of car, with differing power outputs and characteristics, are allowed. The John Cooper Challenge is such a series. It was started in 2002 and became the first ever motor racing series for the New Mini. It is a low cost formula intended for amateur and novice drivers and was created by Mike Cooper in memory of his father John and his involvement with both the old and new Minis. It is a multi-discipline race series based on roadgoing Mini Coopers and Mini Cooper S models race-prepared by John Cooper Motorsport. The cars are bought ready to race. A wide range of competitors have so far taken part, with ages ranging from 18 to over 60.

The John Cooper Challenge is organised by the 750 Motor Club in accordance with the RAC Motors Sports Association (MSA). It is an approved championship and is registered with the MSA.

Following a successful series in 2002 and 2003 which included two hill climbs, one sprint, five sprint races, an overseas race, and a long-distance event, the 2004 championship calendar comprises a similar line-up and includes a sprint, a hill climb, and ten races. This schedule is made up of four sprint races, two UK double-header events, and one double-header race meeting held in mainland Europe. The 12 rounds are run across nine weekends, with a number of them being one-day events The programme is intended to

Right: A rollcage is fitted to the front and rear.

When brake mods are made to race Minis the front crossmember has to be modified to allow the fitting of the brake ducting.

provide a good introduction to a number of different types of motorsport for the beginner and novice driver, as well as offering variety and an added challenge to some of the more experienced competitors.

The roof spoiler fitted to Challenge cars.

Right: Front end treatment of a Cooper Challenge car.

Below right: Racing seats are fitted inside a Challenge car.

Below far right: In all other respects the interior is stripped but standard.

Changes have been made for 2004 in that there are now two classes: the original challenge class for JCW-prepared Mini Coopers, and a new class for the Mini Cooper S. All the competing cars are uprated to Cooper Works or Cooper S Works spec and are fully race-prepared, with a Safety Devices rollcage, and fully uprated suspension and brakes. They are fitted with Dunlop DO1J cut slick tyres, a change that was made in 2003 to cope with the demands of high-speed circuit racing. During the events there is full technical support from John Cooper Motorsport and Dunlop Motorsport.

Ten 140mph, 200bhp Works Cooper Ss have been built for the 2004 Challenge. The existing Cooper Works Club Sport cars have been upgraded to boost the power output from 122 to 133bhp, and the 200bhp Cooper Ss share the grid with the existing Club Class cars. The total number of Minis is being limited to 30 cars across both of the classes so that all the competitors can be accommodated on one grid. Separate championship points are awarded for each class. Points are also awarded for the JCC Novice championship, and at the

end of the season there is an overall champion for the highest number of points scored from either championship. All the cars are sealed and policed at all events to prevent any unauthorised modifications being made.

The cars taking part are built to a road legal specification, meaning that in theory they could be driven to the event (on road tyres), raced, and then driven home again.

Cooper Club Class specification

Engine	4 cylinder, 1,598cc
Max power	130bhp at 6,000rpm
Max torque	118lb ft at 5,000rpm
Power to weight	118bhp per ton
Bore x stroke	85.8 x 77mm
Compression ratio	10.6:1
Gearbox:	Five-speed manual
Final drive	3.94:1.
Front suspension	Bilstein struts, coil springs (height, bump, and rebound adjustable), front anti-roll bar
Rear suspension	Bilstein coil over springs (height, bump, and rebound adjustable), rear anti-roll bar
Steering	Rack and pinion power assisted
Front brakes	273mm vented discs single pot sliding caliper
Front pad material	Mintex 1155, 1166, or F4R
Rear brakes	259mm discs single pot sliding caliper
Rear pad material	Mintex 1144
Wheels	15 x 5.5 alloy
Tyres	Dunlop 195/55/r15 84v semi cut slick
Rollcage	Safety Devices bolt-in six plate with removable side bars, FIA approved
Fire extinguisher	4-litre plumbed in system, manually operated from inside and outside by pull cables, FIA approved
Battery isolator	Electrical cut-out system can be operated from inside and outside of vehicle, MSA approved
Race seat	Corbeau Revolution or Pro Series kevlar compound mix, FIA approved
Seatbelt harness	Luke seat belt harness, five- or six-point fixings, quick release, FIA approved

Mike Cooper's JCW Challenge Mini.

DID YOU KNOW?

The New Mini is an ideal base for a competition car because of its excellent handling and bodyshell stiffness. It has a lot to live up to, though – the BMC Works Rally Team was once listed in the *Guinness Book of Records* as the most successful rally team of all time.

Cooper S Class specification

Engine	4 cylinder, 1,598cc supercharged
Max power	200bhp at 6,950rpm
Max torque	177lb ft at 4,000rpm
Power to weight	175bhp per ton
Bore x stroke	85.8 x 70mm
Compression ratio	8.3:1
Gearbox:	Six-speed Getrag manual
Final drive	2.74:1.
Front suspension	Bilstein struts, coil springs (height, bump, and rebound adjustable), front anti-roll bar
Rear suspension	Bilstein coil over springs (height, bump, and rebound adjustable), rear anti-roll bar
Steering	Rack and pinion power assisted
Front brakes	300mm vented discs alloy four pot caliper
Front pad material	Mintex F4R or 1166
Rear brakes	259mm discs single pot sliding caliper
Rear pad material	Mintex 1144
Hoses	Goodrich braided brake hoses all round
Wheels	Alloy cross spoke 16 x 6.5
Tyres	Dunlop 205/50/r16 87v semi cut slick
Rollcage	Safety Devices bolt-in six plate, with removable side bars, FIA approved
Fire extinguisher	4-litre plumbed in system, manually operated from inside and outside by pull cables, FIA approved
Battery isolator	Electrical cut-out system can be operated from inside and outside of vehicle, MSA approved
Race seat	Corbeau Revolution or Pro Series kevlar compound mix, FIA approved
Seatbelt harness	Luke seat belt harness, five- or six-point fixings, quick release, FIA approved

Top: A Cooper S Challenge car undergoing testing. (John Cooper Works)

Middle: Close competition – JC Challenge Mini Coopers. (John Cooper Works)

Bottom: One-upmanship – flat out around the bend on a hillclimb. (John Cooper Works)

Rallying

A number of privately entered New Minis have taken part in rallying, some in international events, but no works-backed team, nor, as yet, any hint of one in the foreseeable future. Those cars that have competed have proved to be very durable and have emerged virtually unscathed at the end. Preparation for rallying must include suspension modifications using

Mini Challenge cars in action at the Lausitzring in Germany.
(BMW Press)

Keeping the bonnet and bootlid fastened on a rally Mini.

components described in Chapter 11, and a substantial sumpguard, as the Mini has relatively low ground clearance and is very susceptible to damage on rough events. In 2004 Mini specialists Mini Sport announced

An ex-rally John Cooper Works Mini now owned by Jackie Wales. This car is still used in some competitive events.

Mini Sport Rally Championship car undergoing testing. (Mini Sport)

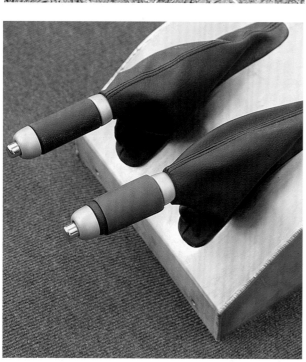

Above left: Rallying calls for special tyres. Steel rims are sometimes used on long events, as they are easier to repair and cheaper.

Above: The full heavy duty sumpguard set that is required for serious rally cars.

Left: A Mini mod that dates back to the 1960s. A fly-off handbrake conversion has been developed.

their own New Mini Rally Championship, to begin in 2005.

The Mini Sport Rally Championship

Mini Sport have been rallying Minis for over 30 years and their new championship is intended to be a low-budget series of ten rallies which will provide some very close competitive motorsport. The Cooper and Cooper S in full rally trim will both be eligible to take part, the former tuned to produce 140bhp and the latter tuned to 200bhp and built to Group N specification.

Ten countries in 12 days – a brief stop on the World Cup Rally 2002.

Both cars will be modified using the Mini Sport upgrade engine components described in Chapter 11. The cars can either be prepared either by Mini Sport or participants can buy the tuning components from the Mini Sport SE range and build the cars themselves. Some other components will be supplied by the series sponsors, and competitors will be able to choose tyres from the Yokohama range. All self-built cars will be scrutineered by Mini Sport.

Competitors in the championship can be of any skill level, with novice drivers competing in the Cooper and more experienced drivers taking part in the S. The Challenge is to run parallel to a minimum of seven rounds of the British National Championship and there will be four gravel and three tarmac events. As well as competing in either the Cooper or Cooper S categories, participants will also contend for overall BNC honours. Mini Sport have already built and tested a car in preparation for building or providing the parts for all the cars which will be competing.

In 2002 a team of three New Mini Coopers entered the World Cup Rally. The rally started at Blenheim Palace, in Oxfordshire, and finished twelve days later in Athens, having taken in ten countries en route. The rally recreated the spirit of the World Cup rallies of the 1970s. It followed a route which took in the best sections of the Alpine Rally and some of the mountain passes from the Liège-Sofia-Liège event, and then joined up with the testing competitive sections of the 2002 Acropolis Rally.

The regulations were tough and tuning and modifications were restricted, the idea being to encourage as many newcomers as possible to take part. The fact that New Minis were entered meant that newcomers included cars as well as drivers! Rally conditions in places were demanding and it is a credit to the three Coopers that they all finished, also that very few problems were encountered along the way.

Back in action, much rough terrain was encountered.

They even managed to notch up a class win in the process. Tuning was in the form of the John Cooper Works Conversion with additional upgrading of the suspension and added underbody protection.

The three Minis involved are today back in Britain and still in use. The car pictured here, No 51, is unscathed apart from some roughening of the plastic sill finishers. A very promising start.

Appendix A

Specifications and performance figures

Dimensions, all models

Body

Number of doors	3
Number of seats	4
Length	3,626mm (Cooper S 3,655mm)
Width	1,688mm
Height (unladen)	1,413mm (Cooper 1,416mm)
Wheelbase	2,467mm
Track	front – 1,458mm
	(Cooper S 1,453mm)
	rear – 1,466mm
	(Cooper S 1,460mm)
Steering	Electro hydraulic power assisted
Turning circle	10.66m
Fuel tank capacity	50l approx
Boot volume	150l

Chassis and suspension

Front suspension	Single-joint McPherson spring strut axle with anti dive
Rear suspension	Longitudinal arms with centrally-pivoted track control arms, Z-axle
Brakes	front – Discs, vented, 276 x 22mm
	rear – Discs, 259 x 10mm

Mini One

Capacity	1,598cc
Compression ratio	10.6:1
Bore/stroke	77/85.8mm
Max output	90bhp @ 5,500rpm
Max torque	140Nm @ 3,000rpm
0–62mph	10.9 seconds (12.7 CVT)
50–75mph in 4th gear	12.8 seconds
Top speed	112mph (106 CVT)
Power-to-weight ratio DIN	15.8kg/kW
Output per litre	41.3kW
Urban fuel consumption	32.5mpg (25.9 CVT)
Extra urban fuel consumption	54.3mpg (47.9 CVT)
Combined fuel consumption	43.5mpg (36.7 CVT)
CO_2 emissions	158g/km (187 CVT)
Emission classification	EU 4
Battery	46Ah
Alternator	105/120A/W
Transmission	Five-speed-manual
Gear ratios	1st – 3.417:1
	2nd – 1.947:1
	3rd – 1.333:1
	4th – 1.054:1
	5th – 0.846:1
	reverse – 3.580:1
Final drive	3.556:1 (4.05 CVT)
Tyres	175/65R15
Wheels	15in steel
Weight	1,140kg (1,155 CVT)

Mini One D

Capacity	1,364cc
Compression ratio	18.5:1
Bore/stroke	73/81.5mm
Max output	75bhp @ 4,000rpm
Max torque	180Nm @ 2,000rpm
0–62mph	13.8 seconds
50–75mph in top gear	12.3 seconds
Top speed	103mph
Power-to-weight ratio DIN	19.3kg/kW
Output per litre	40.3kW
Urban fuel consumption	48.7mpg
Extra urban fuel consumption	65.7mpg
Combined fuel consumption	58.9mpg
CO_2 emissions	129g/km
Emission classification	EU 3

Battery	70Ah
Alternator	130/130/A/W
Transmission	Six-speed manual
Gear ratios	1st – 12.57:1
	2nd – 6.99:1
	3rd – 4.51:1
	4th – 3.55:1
	5th – 3.05:1
	6th – 2.41:1
	reverse – 11.13:1
Tyres	175/65R15
Wheels	15in steel
Weight	1,175kg

Mini Cooper

Capacity	1,598cc
Compression ratio	10.6:1
Bore/stroke	77/85.8mm
Max output	115bhp @ 6,000rpm
Max torque	149Nm @ 4,500rpm
0–62mph	9.2 seconds (10.4 CVT)
50–75mph in 4th gear	10.5 seconds
Top speed	124mph (115 CVT)
Power-to-weight ratio DIN	12.4kg/kW
Output per litre	53.2kW
Urban fuel consumption	31.0mpg (25.9 CVT)
Extra urban fuel consumption	52.3mpg (47.9 CVT)
Combined fuel consumption	41.5mpg (36.7 CVT)
CO_2 emissions	163g/km (187 CVT)
Emission classification	EU 4
Battery	46Ah
Alternator	105/120A/W
Transmission	Five-speed manual
Gear ratios	1st – 3.417:1
	2nd – 1.947:1
	3rd – 1.333:1
	4th – 1.054:1
	5th – 0.846:1
	reverse – 3.580:1
Final drive	3.937:1 (4.05 CVT)
Tyres	175/65R15
Wheels	15in alloy
Weight	1,150kg (1,165 CVT)

Mini Cooper S

Capacity	1,598cc
Compression ratio	8.3:1
Bore/stroke	77/85.8mm
Max output	115bhp @ 6,000rpm
Max torque	163Nm @ 6,000rpm

0–62mph	7.4 seconds
50–75mph in 4th gear	6.7 seconds
Top speed	135mph
Power-to-weight ratio DIN	9.3kg/kW
Output per litre	75.1kW
Urban fuel consumption	24.8mpg
Extra urban fuel consumption	41.5mpg
Combined fuel consumption	33.6mpg
CO_2 emissions	202g/km
Emission classification	EU 4
Battery	55Ah
Alternator	105/120A/W
Transmission	Six-speed manual
Gear ratios	1st – 11.425:1
	2nd – 7.181:1
	3rd – 5.397:1
	4th – 4.407:1
	5th – 3.656:1
	6th – 2.986:1
	reverse – 11.13:1
Final drive	2.74:1
Tyres	195/65R16
Wheels	16in alloy
Weight	1,140kg

All figures are quoted from New Mini technical data sheets.

Mini colours

The standard Mini colours are:

Black
Chili Red
Liquid Yellow
Pepper White

The metallic colours are:

British Racing Green
Cosmos Black
Indi Blue
Pure Silver
Solid Gold
Electric Blue
Dark Silver

Following the introduction of the Mini Convertible in July 2004 two new metallic exterior paint colours became available: Astro Black (replaces Cosmos Black) and Black-Eyed Purple (replaces Indi Blue). Another new metallic colour, Hyper Blue, is reserved for Cooper

S models, while Electric Blue was extended as a colour option on all models with the exception of the Mini Convertible. This means that there is a choice of ten exterior colours for every Mini in the range.

Interior improvements introduced July 2004

All models received the following ergonomic improvements:

New storage area
New coin tray area under the handbrake
Larger rear cup-holder
Door armrest with improved ergonomic grip
More spacious door bin for improved storage
Additional side-mounted sun visor for driver
Improved side support from seat bench side bolsters
Addition of passenger grab handle above window
Larger rear-view mirror
Clock repositioned from headlining to central instrument panel
Improved interior ambient lighting
ISOFIX and CD preparation as standard
Rev counter (previously not standard on Mini One)

Upholstery options have increased to 14 different cloth, cloth/leather and full leather designs. Cloth Dragon replaces Cloth Aqua as the standard upholstery for the Mini One and Mini One D, and Cloth Octagon replaces Cloth Kaleido as standard on Mini Cooper models. A new body-coloured trim increases the choices of Mini Cooper S interior trim to five, the other available colours being Chili Red, Liquid Yellow, Electric Blue, and Hyper Blue. Alternatively customers can choose from silver, anthracite, alloy patina, and wood.

There are also some technical modifications and performance improvements. From July 2004 all Mini One and Mini Cooper models came with a new five-speed Getrag gearbox with modified gear ratios, resulting in improved acceleration for both models. Torque on the Mini Cooper went up from 149Nm to 150Nm at 4,500rpm, knocking 0.1 of a second off the previous 0–62mph time of 9.2 seconds. Acceleration from 50–75mph in fifth gear was one second faster at 13.5 seconds. Power output on the Cooper S also went up by 7bhp, bringing it to 170bhp at 6,000rpm, and the top speed increased by 3mph to 138mph. The 0–62mph time reduced by 0.2 seconds to 7.2 seconds.

Viper stripes that go over the bonnet, roof, and back of the car.

New Mini specialists

Avonbar Racing, Avcon House, Bullocks Farm,
Bullocks Lane, Takely, Essex, CM22 6TA.
Tel: 01279 873428. Fax: 01279 873427.
Website: www.avonbar.com.

Peter Baldwin Rolling Road Engine Tuning,
Wilsher Garages Ltd, 18 Cambridge Road, Wimpole,
Cambs, SG8 5QE. Tel: 01223 207217.
Fax: 01223 207996.

Birds, Iver Lane, Uxbridge, Middlesex, UB8 2JF.
Tel: 01895 810850. Website: www.birdsauto.com.

Carburation and Injection Tuning Ltd,
Rolling Road Tuning, Unit 2, 36 Sutton Road,
Coxside, Plymouth, PL4 0JE. Tel: 01752 256262.

Carrozzeria Castagna, Tel: 0039 02 4548 0260.
Website: www.carrozzeriacastagna.com.

Cobra Superform Limited, Units D1 and D2,
Halesfield 23, Telford, TF7 4NY. Tel: 01952 684020.
Website: www.cobraseats.com.

Cool New Ltd, Unit 6, 177–181 Hornchurch Road,
Hornchurch, Essex, RM12 4TE. Tel: 01708 471123.
Website: www.coolnew.co.uk.

John Cooper Works, North Lane, East Preston,
West Sussex, BN16 1BN. Tel: 01903 784784.
Fax: 01903 787722.
E-mail: works@johncooper.co.uk.
Website: www.johncooper.co.uk.

Cooper Turbo Research & Development Inc,
139 N Pacific Street (Suite A-1), San Marcos,
CA 92069, USA. Tel: 760 591 0311.

Green Cotton Air Filters, Auto Inparts Ltd, Unit L2,
Cherrycourt Way Industrial Estate, Stanbridge Road,
Leighton Buzzard, Bedfordshire, LU7 4UH.
Tel: 01525 382713.

Induction Technology Group Ltd, Unit 5, Fairfield Court,
Seven Stars Industrial Estate, Whitley, Coventry,
CV3 4LJ. Tel: 02476 305386.

Kent Performance Camshafts, Units 1–4, Military Road,
Shorncliffe Industrial Estate, Folkestone, Kent,
CT20 3SP. Tel: 01303 248666.
E-mail: kentcams@BTinternet.com.

K&N Filters (Europe) Ltd, John Street, Warrington,
Cheshire, WA2 7UB. Tel: 01925 636950.

Mini Spares Centre, Cranbourne Industrial Estate,
Cranbourne Road, Potters Bar, Herts, EN6 3JN.
Tel: 01707 607700. Fax: 01707 656786.
E-mail: spares@minispares.com.

Mini Spares Midlands, 991 Wolverhampton Road,
Oldbury, West Midlands, B69 4RJ. Tel: 0121 544 0011.
Fax: 0121 544 0022.

Mini Spares North, Unit 6, Freemans Way,
Harrogate Business Park, Harrogate, North Yorks,
HG3 1DH. Tel: 01483 881800. Fax: 01428 881801.

Mini Spares South, 3 Crane Street, Cranbourne,
Dorset, BH21 5QD. Tel: 01725 517999.
Fax: 01725 517878.

Mini Speed, Units 4–5, Abbot Close, Oyster Lane,
Byfleet, Surrey, KT14 7JN. Tel: 01932 400567.
Fax: 01932 400565. E-mail: sales@minispeed.co.uk.

Mini Sport Ltd, Thompson Street, Padiham, Lancs,
BB12 7AP. Tel: 01282 778731.

Moss London, Hampton Farm Industrial Estate,
Hanworth, Middlesex, TW13 6DB. Tel: 0208 867 2020.
Website: www.moss-mini.co.uk. Branches
throughout UK.

Newton Commercial, Eastlands Industrial Estate,
Leiston, Suffolk, IP16 4LL. Tel: 01728 832880.
Fax: 01728 832881.
E-mail: newtoncomm@anglianet.co.uk.
Website: www.newtoncomm.co.uk.

Piper Cams, 2 St John's Court, Ashford Business Park,
Sevington, Ashford, Kent, TN24 0SJ.
Tel: 01233 500200. Fax: 01233 500300.

Pipercross Performance Air Filters, Units 4–6,
Tenter Road, Moulton Park Industrial Estate,
Northampton, NN3 6PZ. Tel: 01604 494945.

P&L Minis, 34 High Street, Thurnscoe, Rotherham,
South Yorks, S63 0SU. Tel: 01709 889922.
Website: www.plmini.com.

R.T. Quaife Engineering Ltd, Vestry Road, Otford,
Sevenoaks, Kent, TN14 5EL. Tel: 01732 741144.
Fax: 01732 741555. Website: www.quaife.co.uk.

Southern Carburettors and Injection, Unit 6,
Nelson Trading Estate, Morden Road, Wimbledon,
London, SW19 3BL. Tel: 0208 540 2723.
Fax: 0208 540 0857.

Tech Del Ltd (Minilite Wheels), Unit 8A,
Roughmoor Industrial Estate, Williton, Taunton,
Somerset, TA4 4RF. Tel: 01984 631033.
Website: www.minilite.co.uk.

Webasto Hollandia UK Limited, Unit 8D,
Stockton Close, Minworth Industrial Estate,
Sutton Coldfield, Birmingham, B76 1DH.
Tel: 0121 313 1222. Website: www.webasto.co.uk.

West Tuning, Unit 20, Thruxton Race Circuit, Hants,
SP11 8PW. Tel: 01264 773839.
Website: www.west-tuning.com.

Wood and Picket Limited, Unit 14, Faygate
Business Centre, Faygate, Horsham, West Sussex,
RH12 4DN. Tel: 01293 852100. Fax: 01293 852110.
Website: www.woodandpicket.com.

Wherever you view it from the Convertible looks stylish.

Index